RAGA, YOGA AND MANAGEMENT

A READY RECKONER FOR THE YOUNG MANAGERS

DR. PARTHA PRIYA DAS & DR. MONI DEEPA DAS

PARTRIDGE

Copyright © 2024 by DR. PARTHA PRIYA DAS & DR. MONI DEEPA DAS.

ISBN:	Softcover	978-1-5437-0978-0
	eBook	978-1-5437-0977-3

All rights reserved. No part of this book may be used or reproduced by any means, graphic, electronic, or mechanical, including photocopying, recording, taping or by any information storage retrieval system without the written permission of the author except in the case of brief quotations embodied in critical articles and reviews.

Because of the dynamic nature of the Internet, any web addresses or links contained in this book may have changed since publication and may no longer be valid. The views expressed in this work are solely those of the author and do not necessarily reflect the views of the publisher, and the publisher hereby disclaims any responsibility for them.

Print information available on the last page.

To order additional copies of this book, contact
Partridge India
000 800 919 0634 (Call Free)
+91 000 80091 90634 (Outside India)
orders.india@partridgepublishing.com

www.partridgepublishing.com/india

CONTENTS

Preface vii

Chapter 1   Saga of Today's Managers 1
Chapter 2   The Power of Music...48
Chapter 3   Classical Music and Its Elements 72
Chapter 4   A Glimpse Into Hindustani Classical Music 109
Chapter 5   'Chakras' And 'Ragas'.....................................126
Chapter 6   Music and Stress Relief..................................144
Chapter 7   Practical Application of the Book...................186

About the Author 195

PREFACE

How Learning Music Makes a Person a Successful Entrepreneur?

Perhaps surprisingly, a successful entrepreneur will often share attributes with musicians and music lovers. For example, a lot of famous and successful people are musically gifted. There's Paul Allen, cofounder of Microsoft. Roger McNamee, founder of Silver Lake Partners and Elevation Partners. Even Steve Wozniak, cofounder of Apple, is a performing musician. Music has some pretty clear ties to success, and by learning what those ties are a person can turn him/her love of the art form into a way to benefit him/her as a successful entrepreneur.

A musician or a true fan of music has to be an attentive listener to earn one of those titles. By listening for specific beats and riffs on a track, a person can piece together why a song is of a high or low quality. Likewise, a successful entrepreneur knows how to separate the good from the bad. By listening closely to others' ideas, they can dissect what parts work and what parts don't. That ability to compartmentalize is a key attribute of musicians, fans of music and successful entrepreneurs alike. Therefore listening music makes a person a better listener.

Musicians absolutely dedicate themselves to their craft in order to reap big rewards. Far before they're partying like rock stars they're earning their way to that rock star status through hard work and impressive displays of discipline. In the same way an emerging talent transforms into a bestselling artist, take the time to build new skills and hone the skills you already have so that you can become a successful entrepreneur. This practice of music makes a person more disciplined.

A good musician, or even someone fond of making quality mix tapes, understands the importance of experimentation. They have to be willing to get their hands dirty in order to discover sounds that nobody else has imagined or to come up with a compilation of tracks that produce unique experiences. A successful entrepreneur has to similarly find new ways to mesh things together and come up with fresh perspectives. A great business solves a problem, so a successful entrepreneur has to be someone who is willing to experiment until they figure out the problem they can profit from solving. So by practicing music a person learns to do experiment.

Music makers and music lovers alike need to collaborate with others to reach their peak potential. Even the best singer benefits greatly from a back-up band, and making mixes is all about sharing your love of music with others. A successful entrepreneur equally benefits from smart people by their side. You can get pretty far on your own as a businessman or businesswoman, but you really need the advice and wisdom of others to maximize your opportunities for success. So music listeners are became more collaborative.

Musicians spend most of their time touring, and the most passionate music fans will often follow them on the road. Through their travels they learn to brave new environments and find ways to live on less. A successful entrepreneur also has to be prepared for sometimes uncomfortable experiences as well as the lean times inevitable for even the most impressive businesses. So the person gets used to life "on the road".

Learning music can significantly contribute to the development of skills and traits essential for entrepreneurial success. Firstly, the discipline and perseverance gained through regular practice and long-term commitment to mastering an instrument mirror the dedication required to build and sustain a successful business. This rigorous practice routine fosters a strong sense of discipline and the ability to persist through challenges, both crucial for entrepreneurs facing the ups and downs of business ventures.

Creativity and innovation are also nurtured through musical training. Musicians constantly engage in creative processes, whether composing new pieces or interpreting existing ones. This creativity translates into innovative thinking in entrepreneurship, aiding in the development of unique products, services, and solutions. Moreover, the problem-solving skills honed through composing and improvising music are vital for navigating the complexities of business.

Teamwork and collaboration are inherent in ensemble playing, where musicians learn to work effectively in a team, listen to others, and contribute to a collective goal. These experiences enhance an entrepreneur's ability to collaborate with co-founders, employees, and stakeholders. Additionally, the communication skills developed through music—both non-verbal and emotional expression—are invaluable for leadership and negotiation in business.

Attention to detail is another critical skill developed through musical performance, which demands precision in reading notes and maintaining rhythm. This meticulousness is beneficial for entrepreneurs when managing finances, operations, and customer relations. Furthermore, adaptability and flexibility are key traits cultivated through musical improvisation, which teaches musicians to adapt on the fly during performances. Entrepreneurs benefit from this adaptability when they must pivot their strategies in response to market changes and unforeseen challenges. The resilience and ability to learn from mistakes, emphasized in musical training, are also crucial traits for any entrepreneur.

Emotional intelligence, enhanced through the emotional expression and understanding inherent in music, is vital for managing teams, understanding customer needs, and building strong relationships. Musicians' ability to express and understand emotions translates into higher empathy and emotional intelligence in business contexts. Additionally, the cognitive benefits of learning music, such as improved memory and cognitive functions, enhance an entrepreneur's ability to remember details, think strategically, and process complex information efficiently.

Finally, confidence and the ability to perform in public are nurtured through musical performances. Performing in front of an audience builds confidence and reduces fear of public speaking, skills that are essential for entrepreneurs who need to pitch ideas, present to investors, and speak at conferences. In summary, learning music equips individuals with a diverse set of skills and traits—discipline, creativity, teamwork, attention to detail, adaptability, emotional intelligence, cognitive abilities, and confidence—that are integral to entrepreneurial success. These attributes not only help in managing a business but also in innovating and leading effectively in the dynamic world of entrepreneurship.

A person, being a musician, probably not going to start his career performing in a concert at Albert Hall in London. More likely, he is going to be opening for a small local band at a small, sparsely-attended club. And that's okay. He has to work his way up the ladder in order to be either a best-selling musician or a leader in business. Knowing the long shots of becoming a successful recording artist helps you appreciate the somewhat better odds of becoming a successful entrepreneur. Therefore a music learner learns that success takes time.

Following are the reasons why people who learn music are more likely to be successful:

People who learn music are more likely to be successful due to the diverse set of skills and attributes they develop through their musical education. Firstly, the discipline required for regular practice instills a strong work ethic and perseverance, essential traits for achieving long-term goals in any field. This consistent effort and dedication help individuals tackle challenges with resilience and maintain focus on their objectives. Furthermore, the creativity fostered through composing and interpreting music translates into innovative thinking and problem-solving abilities, enabling individuals to develop unique solutions and adapt to changing circumstances.

In addition to creativity, musical training enhances teamwork and collaboration skills. Playing in ensembles teaches individuals to work harmoniously with others, listen actively, and contribute effectively to a collective goal, all of which are crucial for success in professional environments. The attention to detail required in musical performance, from reading notes accurately to maintaining rhythm, sharpens one's ability to manage intricate tasks and ensures precision in their work.

Adaptability and flexibility, cultivated through improvisation and performance, allow musicians to thrive in dynamic situations and pivot strategies when necessary, a key component of success in rapidly evolving industries. Emotional intelligence is another significant benefit, as musicians learn to express and understand emotions deeply, fostering empathy and strong interpersonal skills. This ability to connect with others on an emotional level enhances leadership, teamwork, and customer relations.

Cognitive benefits such as enhanced memory and improved cognitive functions further contribute to an individual's success, allowing them to process complex information efficiently and recall important details. Finally, the confidence gained from performing in public builds the self-assurance needed to present ideas compellingly and navigate high-pressure situations effectively. Overall, the comprehensive skill set developed through learning music equips individuals with the discipline, creativity, teamwork, attention to detail, adaptability, emotional intelligence, cognitive abilities, and confidence that significantly increase their likelihood of success in various endeavours.

Nowadays however, there is a mountain of evidence suggesting that music education is not only good for you, but nearly essential if you want to be successful in life.

What is it about musicians that give them an edge over others?

a. They Are More Creative
b. Their Brains Develop Differently
c. They Connect With Others Better
d. They Are Better at Maths
e. They Have a Better Sense of Rhythm
f. They Are Obsessive
g. They Are More Likely To Have a Higher IQ
h. They Process Speech More Efficiently
i. They Are Conditioned To Work Hard For Results
j. They Have More Self-Control.

The above things happens because Music is an outlet for creativity and self-expression, a tool for self-discipline, a uniting force, promotes responsibility and self-esteem, beneficial to the community, boosts a student's cognitive ability and lastly it is universal.

Following are the reasons why people should listen to more Classical Music

1. It makes brain work better
2. It helps people with dementia
3. It can help people sleep better.
4. It can calm a person down when driving
5. It can help reduce pain
6. It can help person to express emotions
7. It can help blood pressure
8. It can help people on diets

Classical music, with its rich history and intricate compositions, offers numerous benefits that make it an essential part of one's listening repertoire. Firstly, the cognitive benefits of classical music are well-documented. Listening to composers like Mozart, Bach, and Beethoven can stimulate brain function, enhance memory, and improve spatial-temporal reasoning. This phenomenon, often referred to as the "Mozart Effect," suggests that exposure to complex musical structures can boost intellectual capabilities, particularly in children. Studies have shown that students who listen to classical music while studying or before exams tend to perform better academically, as the music helps to enhance concentration and retention of information.

Moreover, classical music has profound effects on mental health and emotional well-being. The soothing melodies and harmonies can reduce stress, anxiety, and depression. The slow tempos and harmonious progressions of pieces like Debussy's "Clair de Lune" or Chopin's Nocturnes create a calming environment that promotes relaxation and tranquillity. Listening to classical music has been found to lower blood pressure and decrease levels of cortisol, the stress hormone. This makes it an effective tool for stress management and overall emotional health. Additionally, classical music's ability to evoke a wide range of emotions can provide listeners with a healthy outlet for processing their feelings, leading to improved emotional regulation.

Classical music also enhances creativity and problem-solving skills. The complex and varied structures of classical compositions encourage listeners to think abstractly and approach problems from multiple perspectives. This is particularly beneficial for those in creative fields or any profession that requires innovative thinking. By engaging with the intricate patterns and themes in classical music, listeners can develop a greater capacity for creative thought and innovative problem-solving.

Social and cultural enrichment is another significant reason to listen to classical music. Understanding and appreciating classical music can provide a deeper connection to the cultural and historical contexts in which these works were created. This knowledge enriches one's understanding of history, literature, and art, fostering a greater appreciation for the cultural achievements of the past. Additionally, classical music often serves as a gateway to other forms of art and culture, inspiring a lifelong interest in learning and cultural exploration.

Furthermore, classical music offers a unique aesthetic experience that can enhance the quality of life. The beauty and sophistication of classical compositions provide a form of aesthetic pleasure that is both intellectually and emotionally rewarding. Listening to a well-performed symphony or opera can be a deeply moving experience, offering a sense of beauty and transcendence that is difficult to find in everyday life. This aesthetic enjoyment can contribute to a richer, more fulfilling life experience.

On a social level, classical music can also bring people together and foster a sense of community. Attending classical music concerts, whether at grand concert halls or intimate chamber settings, provides opportunities for social interaction and shared cultural experiences. These events often attract diverse audiences, allowing individuals to connect with others who share a passion for music. The communal experience of listening to live classical music can create a sense of unity and shared appreciation that transcends individual differences.

Moreover, classical music education can have lasting benefits for young people. Learning to play an instrument or understanding musical theory enhances discipline, patience, and perseverance. These skills are transferable to many areas of life, including academic and professional pursuits. Children who engage with classical music education often develop better language skills, improved mathematical abilities, and enhanced critical thinking skills. This early exposure to music not only fosters a lifelong appreciation for the arts but also equips young people with valuable skills that contribute to their overall development and success.

Incorporating classical music into daily life can also improve productivity and focus. Many people find that playing classical music in the background while working or studying helps to create a calm and focused environment. The lack of lyrics and the steady tempo of classical music can minimize distractions and enhance concentration, making it an ideal choice for background music in various settings, from offices to study rooms.

In summary, listening to more classical music offers a multitude of benefits that enhance cognitive function, emotional well-being, creativity, social and cultural enrichment, aesthetic pleasure, community building, education, and productivity. The timeless nature of classical music ensures that it continues to provide value and enjoyment to listeners of all ages and backgrounds. By integrating classical music into daily life, individuals can experience these benefits first-hand, leading to a richer, more balanced, and fulfilling life.

Here is a list of some famous western classical music pieces which will help people get off to sleep.

- Johann Sebastian Bach – Air on the G String
- Ludwig van Beethoven – Sonata No. 14 "Moonlight" – First movement
- Frederic Chopin – Berceuse in D flat opus 57
- Claude Debussy – Claire de Lune
- Gustav Mahler – Symphony No. 5 – Adagietto
- Wolfgang Amadeus Mozart – Piano Concerto in C major K 467 – Second movement
- Bela Bartok – Piano Concerto No. 3 – Second movement

Leaving lot of things and matters, the aim of this book is to consider what we know about the ways that transfer can occur in relation to the skills developed through active engagement with music and how they may impact on the intellectual, social and personal development of children and young people. The book synthesizes indicative research findings and considers the implications for education.

This overview provides a strong case for the benefits of active engagement with music, especially Indian classical music throughout the lifespan. In early childhood there seem to be benefits for the development of perceptual skills which effect learning language subsequently impacting on literacy which is also enhanced by opportunities to develop rhythmic co-ordination. Fine motor co-ordination is improved through learning to play an instrument. Music also seems to improve spatial reasoning, one aspect of general intelligence which is related to some of the skills required in mathematics. While general attainment is clearly affected by literacy and numeracy skills, motivation which depends on self-esteem, self-efficacy and aspirations is also important in the amount of effort given to studying. Engagement with music can enhance self-perceptions but only if it provides positive learning experiences which are rewarding. This means that musical experiences need to be enjoyable providing challenges which are also attainable. Teaching needs to generate an environment which is supportive and sufficiently flexible to facilitate the development of creativity and self-expression. Group music making is also beneficial to the development of social skills and can contribute to health and well-being throughout the lifespan and can therefore contribute to community cohesion providing benefits to society as a whole.

CHAPTER 1

Saga of Today's Managers

"Music is a Discipline and a Mistress of Good Manners, she makes the people milder and gentler, more Moral and more Reasonable"
— Martin Luther King.

IMAGINE THAT YOU are a manager, and that you've recently been dealing with a lot of people problems.

It's been another long day.

You're now meeting with your last "client" before you go home.

As you listen to this person, you start to get tense.

You find yourself avoiding making direct eye contact with him/her, and you feel yourself shutting down emotionally.

You don't want to listen to his/her complaints at all; instead, you just want to finish.

Rather than taking your frustrations out on this person, however, you apologize and ask for a five-minute break. You go for a quick walk outside, breathe deeply, and then stop for some water. When you go back into your office, you're smiling, refreshed, and ready to help.

Most people experience some degree of stress in their jobs. But if you understand the most common types of stress and know how to spot them, you can manage your stress much better. This, in turn, helps you to work productively, build better relationships, and live a healthier life.

The four common types of stress are:

1. Time stress.
2. Anticipatory stress.
3. Situational stress.
4. Encounter stress

Let's look at each of these types of stress in detail, and discuss how you can identify each one.

1. *Time Stress*

You experience time stress when you worry about time, or the lack thereof. You worry about the number of things that you have to do, and you fear that you'll fail to achieve something important. You might feel trapped, unhappy, or even hopeless.

Time stress is a pervasive issue that affects individuals across various aspects of their lives, creating a sense of anxiety and urgency around the limited time available to accomplish tasks. This form of stress arises when individuals worry about their ability to manage their responsibilities within the constraints of time. The feeling that there are too many tasks to complete and insufficient time to do so can lead to significant psychological distress. This distress is characterized by a constant sense of rushing and an underlying fear of failure. For many, the day begins with an overwhelming to-do list, and the pressure to meet deadlines or arrive punctually for meetings amplifies this stress. The persistent worry about not meeting expectations, whether self-imposed or external, can make individuals feel trapped in a cycle of urgency and anxiety.

The effects of time stress extend beyond mere inconvenience; they can deeply impact mental and emotional well-being. Individuals experiencing time stress often report feelings of unhappiness and hopelessness. The continuous pressure can lead to burnout, characterized by exhaustion, decreased productivity, and a lack of motivation. This is particularly evident in professional environments where deadlines are stringent and the pace is relentless. Employees may find themselves constantly rushing from one task to another, with little time to pause and reflect, leading to a reduction in the quality of their work and overall job satisfaction.

Moreover, time stress can adversely affect personal relationships and health. When individuals are preoccupied with the ticking clock, they may become irritable or withdrawn, straining relationships with family, friends, and colleagues. The relentless focus on time can also lead to poor health habits, such as inadequate sleep, unhealthy eating patterns, and neglect of physical exercise, all of which can exacerbate the feeling of stress. Over time, these health issues can compound, leading to more severe physical and mental health problems.

The psychological impact of time stress often manifests in a diminished capacity to enjoy life's simple pleasures. Activities that were once sources of joy and relaxation, such as hobbies or spending time with loved ones, can become burdensome when overshadowed by the constant pressure of time constraints. This can create a cycle where the lack of leisure and relaxation further diminishes an individual's ability to cope with stress, leading to increased feelings of despair and entrapment.

One common scenario where time stress is prevalent is in the context of academic or professional deadlines. Students, for example, may experience intense pressure to complete assignments and prepare for exams within tight timeframes. This pressure can lead to sleepless nights and a constant state of anxiety, ultimately affecting their academic performance and mental health. Similarly, professionals facing tight project deadlines may find themselves sacrificing personal time and well-being to meet their work obligations, leading to a precarious work-life balance.

To address time stress effectively, it is crucial to develop time management skills and coping strategies. Techniques such as prioritizing tasks, setting realistic goals, and breaking larger tasks into manageable chunks can help individuals regain a sense of control over their time. Additionally, incorporating regular breaks and leisure activities into daily routines can provide much-needed relief from the constant pressure. Mindfulness and relaxation practices, such as meditation and deep breathing exercises, can also be beneficial in managing the physiological and psychological impacts of time stress.

Incorporating technology judiciously can further aid in mitigating time stress. Tools such as calendar apps, project management software, and reminder systems can help individuals organize their tasks more efficiently and reduce the mental load associated with remembering deadlines and appointments. However, it is important to use these tools in a balanced manner to avoid becoming overwhelmed by constant notifications and alerts, which can ironically contribute to stress.

Organizations and institutions also play a critical role in addressing time stress. By promoting a culture that values work-life balance and recognizes the importance of mental health, employers can help reduce the incidence of time stress among employees. Flexible work arrangements, reasonable deadlines, and supportive management practices can create an environment where individuals feel less pressured by time constraints and more able to manage their responsibilities effectively.

In conclusion, time stress is a significant and multifaceted issue that affects many aspects of an individual's life. It stems from the anxiety about not having enough time to meet one's obligations and the fear of failure. The impact of time stress extends to mental and emotional well-being, personal relationships, and physical health. However, by developing effective time management skills, incorporating relaxation practices, and fostering supportive environments, individuals and organizations can mitigate the negative effects of time stress. Addressing this issue is essential for enhancing overall quality of life and achieving a sustainable balance between various responsibilities and personal well-being.

Common examples of time stress include worrying about deadlines or rushing to avoid being late for a meeting.

2. Anticipatory Stress

Anticipatory stress describes stress that you experience concerning the future. Sometimes this stress can be focused on a specific event, such as an upcoming presentation that you're going to give. However, anticipatory stress can also be vague and undefined, such as an overall sense of dread about the future, or a worry that "something will go wrong."

Anticipatory stress is a prevalent and often debilitating form of stress that arises from concerns about future events or outcomes. Unlike stress that is triggered by immediate pressures or past experiences, anticipatory stress is rooted in the anticipation of what might happen. This type of stress can be focused on a specific upcoming event, such as an important presentation, a job interview, or a significant exam. The anxiety surrounding these events often stems from fear of failure, judgment, or the potential consequences of not meeting expectations. The mind becomes preoccupied with what could go wrong, leading to sleepless nights, difficulty concentrating, and a heightened state of alertness. This relentless focus on future uncertainties can drain an individual's mental and emotional resources long before the anticipated event occurs.

However, anticipatory stress is not always tied to a particular event; it can also manifest as a general sense of unease about the future. This form of stress is characterized by vague, undefined worries that something negative might happen. Individuals experiencing this type of stress often report feelings of dread and a persistent, underlying anxiety that can be difficult to pinpoint or rationalize. The source of this stress might be a fear of the unknown, concerns about one's career trajectory, financial stability, or broader existential anxieties about life's uncertainties. This pervasive sense of unease can significantly impact an individual's quality of life, leading to chronic anxiety, restlessness, and a reduced ability to enjoy the present.

The impact of anticipatory stress extends beyond mental and emotional health, influencing physical well-being as well. Chronic anticipatory stress can lead to physical symptoms such as headaches, muscle tension, digestive issues, and a weakened immune system. The body's stress response, which includes the release of stress hormones like cortisol, is designed to prepare for immediate threats. However, when this response is triggered continuously by future-oriented worries, it can result in long-term health problems. For instance, elevated cortisol levels over prolonged periods can contribute to conditions such as hypertension, cardiovascular disease, and metabolic disorders.

Moreover, anticipatory stress can impair decision-making and problem-solving abilities. When individuals are consumed by worries about potential future scenarios, their ability to think clearly and make rational decisions can be compromised. This is because the mind is preoccupied with hypothetical outcomes rather than focusing on the present moment. As a result, individuals may find it challenging to weigh options effectively, consider the consequences of their actions, or approach problems with a clear and strategic mind-set. This can lead to procrastination, indecisiveness, and ultimately, missed opportunities.

In personal and professional contexts, anticipatory stress can strain relationships and diminish performance. In the workplace, an employee might become overly anxious about upcoming projects or performance reviews, leading to reduced productivity and increased errors. This stress can also spill over into interactions with colleagues, resulting in irritability or withdrawal, which can harm team dynamics and collaboration. In personal relationships, the constant worry about future events can lead to emotional unavailability, where individuals are unable to fully engage with their loved ones, causing misunderstandings and conflicts.

To manage anticipatory stress, it is crucial to develop strategies that help mitigate anxiety and foster a more balanced outlook on the future. One effective approach is to practice mindfulness and meditation, techniques that encourage individuals to focus on the present moment rather than future uncertainties. By cultivating a habit of staying grounded in the present, individuals can reduce the intensity of their worries and gain a clearer perspective on their concerns. Cognitive-behavioral techniques can also be beneficial, as they help individuals identify and challenge irrational thoughts about the future, replacing them with more realistic and constructive thinking patterns.

Setting realistic goals and breaking tasks into manageable steps can also alleviate anticipatory stress. When faced with a daunting future event, it can be helpful to create a structured plan that outlines specific actions and timelines. This approach not only provides a sense of control but also reduces the overwhelming nature of large tasks by focusing on incremental progress. Additionally, engaging in regular physical activity and maintaining a healthy lifestyle can enhance resilience against stress, as exercise is known to reduce anxiety and improve mood through the release of endorphins.

Building a support network is another critical factor in managing anticipatory stress. Sharing concerns with friends, family, or a mental health professional can provide emotional relief and practical advice. Supportive relationships offer a sense of security and validation, helping individuals feel less isolated in their worries. Professional counselling or therapy can be particularly effective in addressing deep-seated anxieties and developing personalized coping strategies.

Organizations and workplaces can also play a role in reducing anticipatory stress by fostering environments that prioritize mental health and well-being. Employers can implement policies that encourage work-life balance, provide access to mental health resources, and create a culture of open communication where employees feel comfortable discussing their concerns. By addressing the sources of stress and promoting a supportive atmosphere, organizations can help mitigate the anticipatory stress experienced by their employees, leading to increased job satisfaction and productivity.

Anticipatory stress is a significant and multifaceted issue that arises from concerns about future events or outcomes. It affects mental, emotional, and physical health, and can impair decision-making and interpersonal relationships. However, through mindfulness, cognitive-behavioural techniques, structured planning, physical activity, and strong support networks, individuals can manage this type of stress more effectively. By addressing anticipatory stress proactively, individuals and organizations can enhance well-being, productivity, and overall quality of life.

3. Situational Stress

You experience situational stress when you're in a scary situation that you have no control over. This could be an emergency. More commonly, however, it's a situation that involves conflict, or a loss of status or acceptance in the eyes of your group. For instance, getting laid off or making a major mistake in front of your team are examples of events that can cause situational stress.

Situational stress is a type of stress triggered by specific, often unexpected circumstances that are beyond an individual's control. These situations can be acutely frightening, such as emergencies or crises, but more commonly, they involve scenarios that threaten an individual's social standing, job security, or sense of belonging. For example, receiving news of a layoff can instantaneously plunge someone into situational stress, as the sudden loss of employment brings financial uncertainty and disrupts their career trajectory. Similarly, making a significant mistake in a professional setting can lead to acute stress, driven by the fear of judgment and loss of respect from colleagues and superiors.

The hallmark of situational stress is the immediate and overwhelming nature of the stressor, which often leaves individuals feeling powerless and vulnerable. Unlike chronic stress, which builds over time, situational stress is typically tied to a specific event or series of events. The intense emotional response associated with situational stress can manifest as shock, panic, embarrassment, or humiliation. These emotions can be particularly intense because they often stem from scenarios where individuals feel their personal identity, competence, or social connections are under threat.

One of the most challenging aspects of situational stress is its unpredictability. Unlike other forms of stress that may be anticipated or managed through long-term strategies, situational stress can strike suddenly and with great force. This unpredictability can exacerbate the sense of helplessness and anxiety. For instance, being involved in a car accident, receiving a negative health diagnosis, or encountering a public speaking failure can trigger a cascade of stress responses. These responses include rapid heartbeat, sweating, difficulty breathing, and an overwhelming urge to escape the situation.

Situational stress can significantly impact an individual's mental and physical health if not managed properly. The acute stress response activates the body's fight-or-flight mechanism, releasing a surge of adrenaline and cortisol. While this response is useful in immediate danger, prolonged activation can lead to detrimental health effects such as high blood pressure, compromised immune function, and mental health issues like anxiety and depression. The emotional turmoil of situational stress can also lead to difficulty sleeping, changes in appetite, and a general sense of fatigue and disorientation.

In professional settings, situational stress can impair performance and productivity. For example, an employee who has been publicly criticized by a superior may feel intense stress that hinders their ability to concentrate, make decisions, and interact effectively with colleagues. This not only affects their immediate work output but can also damage their long-term career prospects if the stressor leads to ongoing anxiety or a loss of confidence. Similarly, a student who experiences situational stress from a poor exam performance may struggle with self-doubt and fear of future assessments, affecting their overall academic trajectory.

To cope with situational stress, it is essential to develop effective stress management techniques that can be applied in the moment. One approach is to practice deep breathing exercises and mindfulness, which can help calm the physiological response to stress and bring the mind into the present moment. Cognitive-behavioural strategies can also be beneficial, such as reframing negative thoughts and focusing on problem-solving rather than ruminating on the stressor. For instance, after a public mistake, an individual might remind themselves of their previous successes and formulate a plan to address the error constructively.

Seeking social support is another crucial strategy for managing situational stress. Sharing the stressful experience with trusted friends, family members, or colleagues can provide emotional relief and practical advice. Social support can help individuals feel less isolated and more capable of handling the situation. Professional counselling or therapy can also be valuable, particularly for those who struggle with intense or recurrent situational stress. Therapists can offer coping strategies, stress reduction techniques, and a safe space to process emotions.

Organizations can play a vital role in helping individuals manage situational stress. By fostering a supportive and open workplace culture, employers can reduce the stigma associated with stress and encourage employees to seek help when needed. Providing resources such as employee assistance programs, stress management workshops, and access to mental health professionals can equip employees with the tools they need to handle situational stress effectively. Additionally, clear communication and fair conflict resolution practices can mitigate the impact of stressful events and help maintain a positive work environment.

Preventive measures can also reduce the likelihood of experiencing situational stress. For example, regular training in crisis management and conflict resolution can prepare individuals to handle emergencies and interpersonal conflicts more effectively. Building resilience through ongoing personal development, stress management practices, and maintaining a healthy work-life balance can also fortify individuals against the impact of sudden stressors. Encouraging a culture of continuous feedback and learning can help individuals view mistakes as opportunities for growth rather than threats to their status.

Situational stress is a powerful and often unpredictable form of stress that arises from specific events or circumstances beyond an individual's control. It can significantly impact mental and physical health, professional performance, and overall well-being. However, by developing effective coping strategies, seeking social support, and fostering supportive environments, individuals and organizations can mitigate the effects of situational stress. Through proactive measures and a commitment to resilience, it is possible to navigate the challenges of situational stress and emerge stronger and more capable.

4. Encounter Stress

Encounter stress revolves around people. You experience encounter stress when you worry about interacting with a certain person or group of people – you may not like them, or you might think that they're unpredictable.

Encounter stress can also occur if your role involves a lot of personal interactions with customers or clients, especially if those groups are in distress. For instance, physicians and social workers have high rates of encounter stress, because the people they work with routinely don't feel well, or are deeply upset.

This type of stress also occurs from "contact overload": when you feel overwhelmed or drained from interacting with too many people.

While everyone experiences different physical and emotional symptoms of stress, it's important to understand how you respond to each one. When you can recognize the type of stress you're experiencing, you can take steps to manage it more effectively.

It is said that "a good manager is born and not made". But it has now been established and accepted that it is through the learning and training process that skilled managers are developed. The good managers are committed and dedicated individuals; highly trained and educated, with personal qualities such as ambition, self-motivation, creativity and imagination, a desire for development of the self and the organization they belong to. All management practices are based on the same set of principles; what distinguishes a successful manager from a less successful one is the ability to put these into practice.

The traditional definitions of management emphasizes that the managers achieve organizational objectives by getting things done through workers. Such a view cannot be accepted today because the employees are educated. They should not be treated as mere commodity or means to achieve certain ends. Their needs and aspirations should be given proper consideration. They must be satisfied to ensure their maximum contribution for the achievement of organizational objectives.

Management is universally necessary in all organizations. It is the force by applying skills that hold everything in a business enterprise together and that set everything in motion. We can now come to the point about the managerial skill.

The skill is the ability to make business decisions and lead subordinates within a company. Three most common skills include: 1) human skills - the ability to interact and motivate; 2) technical skills - the knowledge and proficiency in the trade; and 3) conceptual skills – the ability to understand concepts, develop ideas and implement strategies. Competencies include communication ability, response behaviour and negotiation tactics.

These three skills can be grown by intellectual development. Intellectual development refers to the growth of a person throughout the childhood in such a way that their brain becomes more and more capable of analyzing understanding and evaluating concepts to make sense out of the world around them. A child's intelligence enables him or her to adapt to the various environments. Intellectual growth is rapid in infancy, moderate in childhood, and slows down in youth.

Intellectual development is all about learning. It is about how individuals organize their minds, ideas and thoughts to make sense of the world they live in. Here is some of the many ways that individuals learn.

By trial and error they learn copying, exploring and repeating. By questioning they learn doing, experimenting, talking and by experiencing they learn looking, role play, listening and playing.

Children also learn through the other areas of development. For example, physical development through the senses developed by touching, tasting, listening and playing, and emotional and social development through playing with other children and being with people.

The two main areas of intellectual development are:

Language development and Cognitive development. Language development which helps us to organize thoughts and make sense of the world around us and cognitive development which is about how we use our minds and organizes thinking to understand the world around us. They are closely linked.

Intellectual development milestones:

Under language development area,

    Learning to read which includes,
    Being read to
    Looking at books
    Recognizing a picture
    Linking alphabet symbols linked to picture symbols
    Recognizing combinations of alphabet symbols and linking these to picture symbols
    Reading from 4+ years old

Language includes,

    Crying
    Cooing
    Gurgling
    Babbling
    First words

Language development helps us to organize thoughts and make sense of the world around us. It helps an individual to ask questions and develop simple ideas into more complex ideas. Language development depends upon the child's own pattern of development, their age, and the opportunity to experiment and use language. All individuals have a need to communicate and language is the tool that allows this.

Language develops in two phases and begins at birth.

Pre-linguistic – birth to 12 months

    Unintentional crying
    Intentional crying
    Cooing and gurgling
    Babbling
    First words

Linguistic – 12 – 15 months

First words
Holophrases
Jargon
Telegraphic phrases
Complex sentences

Activities

Need to be:

- Talked to
- Listened to
- Praised
- Encouraged

Helped by:

- Using different intonation
- Speaking clearly
- Speaking slowly
- Always answering
- Listening
- Asking questions
- Correcting nicely
- Being patient

Under cognitive development area,

Problem solving which comprises
Trial and error
Identify the problem
Work out a solution
Predict what might happen

Cognitive development – is about how we use our minds and organizes thinking to understand the world around us. Cognitive development depends upon the child's own pattern of development, the opportunity for playing with toys and games and experiences of activities and events.

Cognitive development includes:

Imagination – being able to picture things when they are not in front of you. Children use their imagination for pretend play, pretend games, to tell stories, when drawing, painting, reading, model making, and dressing up.

Problem solving – the ability to solve simple and difficult problems it follows a set pattern of trial and error identify the problem work out a solution predict what might happen. Activities - shapes in a shape sorter, learning to ride a bicycle.

Creativity – being able to express imaginative ideas in a unique way. Activities - painting, drawing, collage, dance, music, cardboard box toy.

Concepts – putting information into an understandable form. Activities – numbers, colours, shape, time, volume, speed, mass (weight).

Memory - the ability to store and recall information, ideas and events. Activities – questioning, telling or writing about a visit, dates, days of the week.

Concentration – ability to pay attention. Children concentrate more if they are interested in the task/activity. They need to concentrate to be able to store and sort information.

Objects permanence – understanding that something still exists even though it can't be seen. Activities – peek-a-boo, hid and seek, treasure hunt.

Reasoning – understanding that actions have a cause and effect. Activity – play center with push and pull buttons to make a bell ring, a toy pop up.

We can refer Bloom's Classification of Cognitive skills for further reference.

Bloom's Classification of Cognitive Skills

Bloom's levels of cognitive skills are provided in the table below, along with definitions for each skills, and related behaviors. The terms can be used to create student learning outcomes that tap into each of the ability levels.

Bloom's Classification of Cognitive Skills		
Category	**Definition**	**Related Behaviors**
Knowledge	Recalling or remembering something without necessarily understanding, using, or changing it	Define, describe, identify, label, list, match, memorize, point to, recall, select, state
Comprehension	Understanding something that has been communicated without necessarily relating it to anything else	Alter, account for, annotate, calculate, change, convert, group, explain, generalize, give examples, infer, interpret, paraphrase, predict, review, summarize, translate

Application	Using a general concept to solve problems in a particular situation; using learned material in new and concrete situations	Apply, adopt, collect, construct, demonstrate, discover, illustrate, interview, make use of, manipulate, relate, show, solve, use
Analysis	Breaking something down into its parts; may focus on identification of parts or analysis of relationships between parts, or recognition of organizational principles	Analyze, compare, contrast, diagram, differentiate, dissect, distinguish, identify, illustrate, infer, outline, point out, select, separate, sort, subdivide
Synthesis	Reacting something new by putting parts of different ideas together to make a whole.	Blend, build, change, combine, compile, compose, conceive, create, design, formulate, generate, hypothesize, plan, predict, produce, reorder, revise, tell, write
Evaluation	Judging the value of material or methods as they might be applied in a particular situation; judging with the use of definite criteria	Accept, appraise, assess, arbitrate, award, choose, conclude, criticize, defend, evaluate, grade, judge, prioritize, recommend, referee, reject, select, support

Managerial Skills

Management is a challenging job. It requires certain skills to accomplish such a challenge. Thus, essential skills which every manager needs for doing a better management are called as Managerial Skills. The degree of three managerial skills i.e. conceptual skills, human relations skills and technical skills varies from levels of management and from an organization to organization.

The top-level managers require more conceptual skills and less technical skills. The lower-level managers require more technical skills and fewer conceptual skills. Human relations skills are required equally by all three levels of management.

Management is an inherently challenging role, demanding a diverse set of skills to navigate the complexities of organizational operations effectively. These essential capabilities, known collectively as managerial skills, encompass three primary categories: conceptual skills, human relations skills, and technical skills. The proficiency required in each of these areas varies depending on the level of management and the specific context of the organization.

At the top level of management, conceptual skills are paramount. These skills involve the ability to see the organization as a whole, understand how its various parts interrelate, and recognize how the organization fits into the broader industry and economic landscape. Top-level managers use conceptual skills to devise strategies, drive innovation, and steer the organization towards long-term goals. They must be adept at abstract thinking and have a keen insight into complex situations to make decisions that shape the future direction of the company. Their focus is less on the day-to-day operations and more on overarching policies and strategic planning.

Conversely, lower-level managers require a higher degree of technical skills. These skills pertain to the specific knowledge and expertise needed to perform particular tasks or functions within the organization. Technical skills are crucial for frontline managers who oversee the direct execution of tasks and operations. They need to understand the intricacies of the work being performed, whether it's in production, sales, marketing, or any other functional area. This deep technical knowledge enables them to supervise effectively, solve operational problems, and train employees to perform their duties proficiently.

Human relations skills, also known as interpersonal skills, are essential at all levels of management. These skills involve the ability to work with, motivate, and manage people. Effective communication, empathy, conflict resolution, and team building are critical components of human relations skills. Managers at every level must interact with subordinates, peers, and superiors, making these skills vital for fostering a collaborative and productive work environment. Strong human relations skills help managers to build trust, inspire their teams, and maintain high morale, which is crucial for organizational success.

The degree to which these skills are emphasized varies not only by management level but also by organizational context. In a highly technical industry, for example, even top-level managers might need a more substantial technical background. Similarly, in smaller organizations, managers often wear multiple hats, necessitating a blend of conceptual, technical, and human relations skills regardless of their level.

Effective management hinges on a balanced combination of conceptual, human relations, and technical skills, tailored to the specific level of management and organizational context. Top-level managers prioritize conceptual skills to navigate strategic challenges, while lower-level managers focus on technical skills to ensure smooth operational execution. Across all levels, human relations skills are indispensable, enabling managers to lead their teams effectively and maintain a harmonious workplace. By understanding and developing these essential managerial skills, managers can better meet the diverse demands of their roles and contribute to the overall success of their organizations.

1. *Conceptual Skills*

Conceptual skill is the ability to visualize (see) the organization as a whole. It includes Analytical, Creative and Initiative skills. It helps the manager to identify the causes of the problems and not the symptoms. It helps him to solve the problems for the benefit of the entire organization. It helps the manager to fix goals for the whole organization and to plan for every situation. Conceptual skills are mostly required by the top-level management because they spend more time in planning, organizing and problem solving.

Conceptual skills are critical for effective management, particularly at the top levels of an organization. These skills encompass the ability to visualize the organization as a cohesive whole, integrating various parts to understand how they interconnect and impact each other. A manager with strong conceptual skills possesses a blend of analytical, creative, and initiative abilities. Analytical skills enable the manager to dissect complex situations, identify underlying problems, and understand their root causes rather than merely addressing symptoms. This deep analysis is essential for developing effective solutions that benefit the entire organization, ensuring that strategies are not short-sighted but rather holistic and sustainable.

Creativity within conceptual skills allows managers to think outside the box and devise innovative solutions to challenges. This creativity is vital for strategic planning and for seizing new opportunities that can propel the organization forward. Initiative, another key component, empowers managers to proactively address issues before they escalate into more significant problems. It involves a forward-thinking approach where managers anticipate potential obstacles and devise plans to mitigate them.

The importance of conceptual skills is particularly pronounced at the top management level, where the focus is predominantly on planning, organizing, and problem-solving. Top-level managers need to set strategic goals that align with the organization's mission and vision. They must plan for various scenarios, considering long-term implications and preparing the organization to adapt to changing environments. This requires a comprehensive understanding of the organization's internal dynamics and external factors, such as market trends, economic shifts, and technological advancements.

Conceptual skills also facilitate effective communication within the organization. Top managers must convey complex ideas and strategies in a clear and compelling manner, ensuring that all stakeholders understand the overarching goals and their roles in achieving them. This clarity helps in aligning the efforts of different departments and fostering a cohesive organizational culture.

Moreover, these skills are essential for problem-solving on an organizational scale. When faced with significant challenges, top managers rely on their conceptual skills to evaluate all possible solutions, weighing the pros and cons of each. They consider the long-term impacts of their decisions, aiming to implement solutions that support sustainable growth and stability. This strategic foresight distinguishes successful top managers, as they can navigate the organization through complexities and uncertainties.

In essence, conceptual skills are indispensable for top-level managers who are responsible for the strategic direction of the organization. These skills enable them to visualize the big picture, integrate various elements of the organization, and develop comprehensive plans that ensure long-term success. By leveraging analytical, creative, and initiative abilities, top managers can address root causes of problems, innovate, and lead their organizations towards achieving their goals. The development and refinement of conceptual skills are thus crucial for anyone aspiring to excel in top management roles, as these skills underpin the ability to guide the organization through both opportunities and challenges.

2. *Human Relations Skills*

Human relations skills are also called Interpersonal skills. It is an ability to work with people. It helps the managers to understand, communicate and work with others. It also helps the managers to lead, motivate and develop team spirit. Human relations skills are required by all managers at all levels of management. This is so, since all managers have to interact and work with people.

Human relations skills, often referred to as interpersonal skills, are essential for managers at all levels of an organization. These skills enable managers to effectively interact, communicate, and work with others, fostering a collaborative and productive work environment. At the core of human relations skills is the ability to understand and empathize with people, which is crucial for building strong relationships and maintaining a positive organizational culture. Effective managers use these skills to lead their teams, motivate employees, and cultivate a sense of unity and shared purpose within their workforce.

A manager with strong human relations skills can navigate the complexities of human interactions with ease. These skills involve active listening, clear and empathetic communication, and the ability to resolve conflicts constructively. Managers must listen to their team members' concerns, provide feedback, and ensure that everyone feels heard and valued. This builds trust and respect, which are foundational to any successful team.

In addition to communication, human relations skills include the ability to inspire and motivate employees. Managers who can articulate a clear vision and connect it to their team's daily work can boost morale and drive performance. Recognizing and appreciating individual contributions further enhances motivation and encourages a culture of excellence. By understanding the unique strengths and needs of their team members, managers can tailor their approach to maximize each person's potential.

Another critical aspect of human relations skills is the ability to develop and maintain team spirit. Managers must create an environment where teamwork is encouraged, and collaboration is the norm. This involves fostering an inclusive atmosphere where diversity is respected, and everyone feels they belong. Team-building activities, open communication channels, and a shared commitment to common goals all contribute to a cohesive team dynamic.

Human relations skills are equally important across all levels of management because all managers, regardless of their hierarchical position, must interact and work with people. For lower-level managers, these skills are crucial for directly supervising and supporting frontline employees. Middle managers rely on interpersonal skills to bridge the gap between upper management's strategic directives and their team's operational execution. Top-level managers use these skills to lead the organization, engage with stakeholders, and ensure that the company's vision and values are communicated effectively throughout the organization.

Moreover, effective human relations skills contribute to a positive organizational climate, reducing turnover and enhancing employee satisfaction. When managers are approachable and supportive, employees are more likely to stay engaged and committed to their work. This leads to higher productivity, better customer service, and ultimately, improved organizational performance.

Human relations skills are indispensable for managers at all levels of an organization. These skills facilitate effective communication, conflict resolution, and team-building, enabling managers to lead and motivate their teams successfully. By fostering strong relationships and a collaborative work environment, managers can enhance employee engagement and drive organizational success. Developing and honing human relations skills is therefore critical for any manager aspiring to lead effectively and create a positive, high-performing workplace.

3. *Technical Skills*

A technical skill is the ability to perform the given job. Technical skills help the managers to use different machines and tools. It also helps them to use various procedures and techniques. The low-level managers require more technical skills. This is because they are in charge of the actual operations.

Technical skills are fundamental abilities that enable managers to perform specific tasks and functions within their role. These skills encompass the practical knowledge and proficiency required to operate machinery, tools, and equipment relevant to the job. Technical skills also involve familiarity with various procedures, techniques, and methodologies essential for executing tasks efficiently and effectively. While technical skills are valuable across all levels of management, they are particularly crucial for lower-level managers who oversee the day-to-day operations of the organization.

Lower-level managers, often referred to as frontline or operational managers, and are directly responsible for supervising the execution of tasks and activities within their department or team. As such, they rely heavily on their technical skills to ensure that operations run smoothly and meet quality standards. For example, a production manager in a manufacturing facility must have a deep understanding of the machinery and processes involved in the production line. Their technical expertise allows them to troubleshoot issues, optimize workflow, and maintain productivity levels.

In addition to operational tasks, technical skills are also essential for managerial functions such as planning, organizing, and controlling. Managers at all levels must be proficient in using relevant software, databases, and analytical tools to gather and analyse data, create reports, and make informed decisions. For instance, a marketing manager may need technical skills in digital marketing platforms, data analytics, and customer relationship management (CRM) software to develop and implement marketing strategies effectively.

While technical skills are indispensable for lower-level managers, they are also valuable for middle and top-level managers, albeit to a lesser extent. Middle managers, who bridge the gap between frontline supervisors and senior executives, require technical skills relevant to their specific department or functional area. For example, an IT manager may need technical expertise in network infrastructure, cyber security, and software development to oversee the organization's technology initiatives.

Similarly, top-level managers benefit from technical skills that enable them to understand the operational aspects of the organization and make informed strategic decisions. While their focus is more on setting goals, formulating policies, and managing resources, top managers must possess a foundational understanding of technical concepts related to their industry or sector. This allows them to communicate effectively with lower-level managers, assess performance metrics, and identify areas for improvement.

Technical skills are essential for managers at all levels of an organization, but their degree of importance varies depending on the managerial role and responsibilities. Lower-level managers rely heavily on technical skills to oversee operational tasks and ensure smooth day-to-day operations. Middle and top-level managers also require technical expertise relevant to their respective departments or functional areas to make informed decisions and effectively lead their teams. By continuously developing and refining their technical skills, managers can enhance their ability to perform their roles proficiently and contribute to the overall success of the organization.

Apart from this three managerial skills, a manager also needs (requires) following additional managerial skills.

4. Communication Skills

Communication skills are required equally at all three levels of management. A manager must be able to communicate the plans and policies to the workers. Similarly, he must listen and solve the problems of the workers. He must encourage a free-flow of communication in the organization.

Communication skills are indispensable for managers at all levels of an organization, from frontline supervisors to top executives. Effective communication is essential for conveying plans, policies, and expectations to employees, ensuring that everyone is aligned with the organization's goals and objectives. Managers must be able to articulate their vision clearly and concisely, whether it involves outlining strategic initiatives or providing instructions for daily tasks.

Moreover, communication is a two-way street, and managers must also be adept listeners, actively engaging with employees to understand their concerns, address their needs, and provide support when necessary. By fostering an environment of open communication, managers encourage transparency, trust, and collaboration, which are essential for maintaining a positive work culture and driving organizational success. Therefore, regardless of their level within the organization, managers must prioritize developing strong communication skills to effectively lead their teams and achieve shared goals.

5. Administrative Skills

Administrative skills are required at the top-level management. The top-level managers should know how to make plans and policies. They should also know how to get the work done. They should be able to co-ordinate different activities of the organization. They should also be able to control the full organization.

Administrative skills are paramount for top-level managers who hold strategic leadership positions within an organization. These skills encompass a range of competencies necessary for effective planning, decision-making, coordination, and control of organizational activities. Top-level managers are responsible for setting the overall direction and vision of the organization, and as such, they must possess the administrative acumen to formulate comprehensive plans and policies that align with the organization's goals and objectives. This involves analysing internal and external factors, forecasting future trends, and identifying strategic opportunities and challenges.

Furthermore, top-level managers must possess the ability to execute these plans effectively by allocating resources, delegating tasks, and overseeing the implementation process. This requires strong organizational skills to coordinate various departments and functions, ensuring that everyone is working towards common objectives. Effective coordination facilitates synergy and efficiency, enabling the organization to maximize its potential and achieve optimal results.

In addition to planning and coordination, top-level managers must also exercise control over the organization to ensure that operations are conducted in accordance with established policies and standards. This involves monitoring performance metrics, assessing progress towards goals, and making necessary adjustments to ensure that objectives are met. Control mechanisms may include financial analysis, performance evaluations, and regular audits to identify areas for improvement and mitigate risks.

Overall, administrative skills are essential for top-level managers to effectively lead and manage the organization. By mastering these skills, top managers can steer the organization towards success, navigate challenges, and capitalize on opportunities in a dynamic business environment. Whether it involves strategic planning, resource allocation, or performance monitoring, top-level managers must possess the administrative proficiency to guide the organization towards its desired outcomes and sustain long-term growth and profitability.

6. *Leadership Skills*

Leadership skill is the ability to influence human behaviour. A manager requires leadership skills to motivate the workers. These skills help the Manager to get the work done through the workers.

Leadership skills are essential for managers at all levels of an organization. Leadership is the ability to inspire and influence others to achieve common goals and objectives. A manager who possesses strong leadership skills can motivate and empower employees to perform at their best, driving productivity, innovation, and organizational success. Effective leadership involves a combination of traits, behaviours, and abilities that enable managers to guide, inspire, and support their teams.

One of the primary functions of leadership is to motivate employees to excel in their roles and contribute to the organization's success. Leaders inspire commitment and dedication by articulating a compelling vision, setting clear goals, and providing purpose and direction to their teams. They create a positive work environment where employees feel valued, supported, and engaged, fostering a sense of ownership and accountability for achieving shared objectives.

Leadership skills also involve the ability to communicate effectively and build strong relationships with team members. Leaders listen actively, seek input from others, and provide constructive feedback to help individuals grow and develop. They communicate openly and transparently, sharing information, goals, and expectations to foster trust and collaboration. By cultivating a culture of communication and collaboration, leaders can harness the collective talents and expertise of their team members to drive innovation and problem-solving.

Furthermore, effective leaders demonstrate integrity, empathy, and emotional intelligence in their interactions with others. They lead by example, modelling ethical behaviour, and holding themselves and others accountable for their actions. Empathy allows leaders to understand and respond to the needs and concerns of their team members, building trust and fostering a supportive work environment. Emotional intelligence enables leaders to manage their own emotions and navigate interpersonal dynamics effectively, leading to stronger relationships and better outcomes.

Leadership skills are not limited to formal managerial roles but can be demonstrated by individuals at all levels of an organization. Whether leading a team, project, or initiative, individuals can leverage their leadership abilities to inspire, influence, and make a positive impact on those around them. By continuously developing and honing their leadership skills, managers can effectively lead their teams through change, adversity, and uncertainty, driving organizational success and creating a culture of excellence.

7. *Problem Solving Skills*

Problem solving skills are also called as Design skills. A manager should know how to identify a problem. He should also possess an ability to find a best solution for solving any specific problem. This requires intelligence, experience and up-to-date knowledge of the latest developments.

Problem-solving skills are essential for managers across all levels of an organization. Often referred to as design skills, these abilities enable managers to identify challenges, analyse underlying causes, and develop effective solutions to address them. A manager proficient in problem-solving possesses the intelligence, experience, and up-to-date knowledge necessary to navigate complex issues and make informed decisions.

The first step in problem-solving is to accurately identify the problem at hand. This requires keen observation, critical thinking, and the ability to gather relevant information. Managers must analyse the situation from multiple perspectives, considering both the symptoms and root causes of the problem. By asking probing questions and conducting thorough research, they can gain a deeper understanding of the issue and its implications for the organization.

Once the problem has been identified, the next step is to generate potential solutions. Effective problem solvers draw upon their creativity, experience, and knowledge to brainstorm innovative ideas and approaches. They consider various alternatives, weighing the pros and cons of each option and evaluating their feasibility and potential impact. Collaborating with team members and seeking input from stakeholders can enrich the problem-solving process, bringing diverse perspectives and insights to the table.

After generating potential solutions, managers must evaluate each option to determine the best course of action. This involves analysing the potential risks, costs, and benefits associated with each alternative and assessing their alignment with organizational goals and values. Managers may use decision-making tools and techniques, such as cost-benefit analysis or risk assessment, to facilitate the evaluation process and make well-informed choices.

Once a decision has been made, managers must implement the chosen solution effectively. This requires strong communication skills to convey the plan to relevant stakeholders, obtain buy-in and support, and coordinate efforts across different departments or teams. Managers must also monitor the implementation process closely, making adjustments as needed and addressing any unforeseen challenges or obstacles that arise.

Finally, managers should evaluate the effectiveness of the solution and its impact on the organization. This involves measuring key performance indicators, soliciting feedback from stakeholders, and assessing whether the problem has been adequately resolved. Continuous learning and improvement are essential aspects of the problem-solving process, as managers seek to apply lessons learned to future challenges and refine their approach over time.

Problem-solving skills are critical for managers to effectively navigate the complexities of the business environment and drive organizational success. By identifying problems, generating creative solutions, and implementing effective strategies, managers can overcome obstacles, seize opportunities, and achieve their goals. Through continuous learning, adaptation, and improvement, managers can enhance their problem-solving abilities and make a meaningful impact on their organizations.

8. *Decision Making Skills*

Decision-making skills are required at all levels of management. However, it is required more at the top-level of management. A manager must be able to take quick and correct decisions. He must also be able to implement his decision wisely. The success or failure of a manager depends upon the correctness of his decisions. In business, we often seem to focus less on good management, and more on the glamorous and exciting work of leadership.

Decision-making skills are indispensable for managers at all levels of an organization, but they are particularly critical for those in top-level management positions. Decision-making involves evaluating various options, weighing potential outcomes, and choosing the course of action that best aligns with organizational goals and objectives. Managers must be able to make quick yet informed decisions, considering both short-term and long-term implications, as well as the potential risks and benefits associated with each option.

Top-level managers, such as CEOs and executive leaders, bear significant responsibility for shaping the strategic direction of the organization through their decisions. They must navigate complex and uncertain business environments, making choices that impact the organization's performance, competitiveness, and sustainability. These decisions may involve setting overarching goals, allocating resources, entering new markets, or restructuring the organization to adapt to changing circumstances.

The success or failure of a manager is often judged by the quality of their decisions. Effective decision-makers demonstrate sound judgment, analytical thinking, and a willingness to take calculated risks. They gather relevant information, consult with key stakeholders, and consider multiple perspectives before reaching a conclusion. Additionally, they possess the confidence and conviction to stand by their decisions, even in the face of uncertainty or criticism.

Implementing decisions wisely is another crucial aspect of decision-making skills. Managers must develop action plans, assign responsibilities, and monitor progress to ensure that decisions are executed effectively. This requires effective communication, delegation, and follow-up to ensure that everyone understands their roles and responsibilities and works together towards achieving the desired outcomes.

Despite its importance, decision-making is not always glamorous or exciting work. It often involves grappling with complex problems, weighing competing priorities, and making tough choices in ambiguous situations. However, effective decision-making is the foundation of good management, as it drives organizational performance and enables the organization to adapt and thrive in a dynamic business environment.

Decision-making skills are essential for managers at all levels of an organization, but they are particularly critical for top-level managers. By making informed, timely decisions and implementing them wisely, managers can drive organizational success and create value for stakeholders. While decision-making may not always be glamorous, it is a fundamental aspect of effective management and leadership, shaping the future direction of the organization and ensuring its long-term viability and success.

However, managers are responsible for making sure that things are done properly. And while leaders may bring us vision, inspiration and challenge, these things count for nothing without the efficient implementation brought about by good management.

To be a great manager, you must have an extensive set of skills – from planning and delegation to communication and motivation. Because the skill set is so wide, it's tempting to build skills in the areas of management that you're already comfortable with. But, for your long-term success, it's wise to analyze your skills in all areas of management – and then to challenge yourself to improve in all of these areas.

Essentials of an Effective Manager

Here I am considering eight essential skill areas where managers should focus their efforts. By covering these basics, you'll enjoy more success as a team manager:

1. Understanding team dynamics and encouraging good relationships.
2. Selecting and developing the right people.
3. Delegating effectively.
4. Motivating people.
5. Managing discipline and dealing with conflict.
6. Communicating.
7. Planning, making decisions, and problem solving.
8. Avoiding common managerial mistakes.

The above eight areas comprising of eight managerial skills i.e. understanding skills, recruiting skills, delegating skills, motivating skills, management skills, communication skills, problem solving and decision making skills and team management skills respectively.

With these skills along with patience and strong sense of balance, you can become a very effective manager.

Understanding team dynamics and fostering positive relationships is foundational to effective management. Managers who grasp the intricacies of team dynamics can create a cohesive and high-performing team environment. This involves recognizing individual strengths and weaknesses, promoting collaboration, and resolving conflicts constructively. By investing in team development and cultivating a culture of trust and mutual respect, managers can harness the collective talents of their team members and achieve greater success.

Selecting and developing the right people is another essential aspect of effective management. Managers must have a keen eye for talent and the ability to recruit, on-board, and train employees who align with the organization's values and goals. Investing in employee development through training programs, mentorship, and career advancement opportunities can enhance employee satisfaction, retention, and performance. By empowering employees to reach their full potential, managers not only strengthen the team but also contribute to the organization's long-term success.

Delegating effectively is crucial for managers to maximize productivity and leverage the talents of their team members. Delegation involves assigning tasks and responsibilities to individuals based on their skills, knowledge, and capabilities. Effective delegation requires clear communication, setting expectations, and providing support and resources as needed. By empowering employees to take ownership of their work and make decisions independently, managers can foster a sense of accountability and autonomy while freeing up time to focus on strategic priorities.

Motivating people is a fundamental skill for managers to inspire and energize their teams. Motivated employees are more engaged, productive, and committed to achieving organizational goals. Managers can motivate their team members by recognizing and rewarding their achievements, providing meaningful feedback and opportunities for growth, and creating a positive work environment where employees feel valued and appreciated. By understanding individual motivators and tailoring their approach accordingly, managers can inspire a culture of excellence and drive performance.

Managing discipline and addressing conflicts are inevitable challenges for managers. Effective managers must be able to enforce organizational policies and standards while fostering a fair and respectful workplace. This involves addressing performance issues promptly, providing constructive feedback, and implementing corrective measures when necessary. Additionally, managers must have the skills to resolve conflicts and mediate disputes among team members, promoting open communication and collaboration to find mutually beneficial solutions.

Communication is a cornerstone of effective management. Managers must be able to articulate their vision, goals, and expectations clearly and consistently to ensure alignment and understanding among team members. This includes both verbal and written communication, as well as active listening and feedback mechanisms to foster open dialogue and collaboration. By mastering communication skills, managers can build trust, resolve conflicts, and facilitate teamwork, ultimately driving organizational success.

Planning, decision-making, and problem-solving are critical competencies for managers to navigate complex and dynamic business environments. Managers must be able to set strategic objectives, develop actionable plans, and make informed decisions based on data and analysis. This requires a blend of analytical thinking, creativity, and risk management to identify opportunities, mitigate challenges, and adapt to changing circumstances. By honing their planning and decision-making skills, managers can anticipate future trends, capitalize on opportunities, and steer the organization towards success.

Avoiding common managerial mistakes is essential for maintaining credibility and effectiveness as a manager. Managers must be aware of common pitfalls such as micromanaging, playing favourites, or failing to provide adequate feedback and support. By learning from past mistakes and continuously seeking feedback and self-improvement, managers can enhance their leadership skills and build trust and confidence among their team members.

In conclusion, effective management requires a diverse set of skills and competencies across various areas, from understanding team dynamics to decision-making and problem-solving. By focusing on these essentials, managers can cultivate high-performing teams, drive organizational success, and achieve their professional goals. Through continuous learning, practice, and self-reflection, managers can become more effective leaders and make a meaningful impact on their organizations and teams.

Now I am exploring each of these eight essential skill areas in more detail.

1. Understanding Team Dynamics and Encouraging Good Relationships

Good management means understanding how teams operate. It's worth remembering that teams usually follow a certain pattern of development: forming, norming, storming, and performing. It's important to encourage and support people through this process; so that you can help your team becomes fully effective as quickly as possible.

When forming teams, managers must create a balance so that there's a diverse set of skills, personalities, and perspectives. You may think it's easier to manage a group of people who are likely to get along, but truly effective teams invite many viewpoints and use their differences to be creative and innovative.

Understanding team dynamics and fostering good relationships among team members is essential for effective management. Teams typically go through stages of development, including forming, norming, storming, and performing. As a manager, it's crucial to support your team through these stages to ensure they become fully effective as quickly as possible.

During the forming stage, managers must create a balanced team with a diverse mix of skills, personalities, and perspectives. While it may seem easier to manage a homogeneous group, truly effective teams thrive on diversity and leverage different viewpoints to drive creativity and innovation. As a manager, your role is to develop the skills necessary to steer these differences in a positive direction.

Introducing a team charter can be a valuable tool for setting expectations and establishing guidelines for how team members will work together. A team charter outlines the team's purpose, goals, roles, and responsibilities, fostering clarity and alignment from the outset. By involving team members in the development of the charter, managers can encourage ownership and commitment to the team's success.

Additionally, knowing how to resolve team conflicts is essential for managing teams effectively. Conflict is a natural part of any team dynamic and can arise from differences in opinion, communication styles, or competing priorities. As a manager, it's important to address conflicts promptly and constructively, creating a safe space for open communication and collaboration. Active listening, empathy, and mediation skills are valuable tools for resolving conflicts and building stronger relationships among team members.

Ultimately, effective management of team dynamics involves creating an environment where diversity is celebrated, communication is open and transparent, and conflicts are addressed proactively and constructively. By fostering a culture of trust, respect, and collaboration, managers can empower their teams to achieve their goals and maximize their potential.

Here, your task is to develop the skills needed to steer those differences in a positive direction. This is why introducing a team charter and knowing how to resolve team conflict is so useful for managing your team effectively.

2. Selecting and Developing the Right People

Finding great new team members and developing the skills needed for your team's success is another important part of team formation.

Selecting and developing the right people is a critical aspect of building a successful team. As a manager, your ability to recruit top talent and nurture their skills and abilities directly impacts your team's effectiveness and overall success.

Improving your recruiting skills is essential for identifying candidates who not only possess the required qualifications but also align with the team's culture and values. Utilizing effective interviewing techniques, such as asking insightful questions that probe candidates' experience, skills, and fit for the role, can help you assess their suitability for the position. Additionally, tools like inbox assessments, recruitment tests, and aptitude testing can provide valuable insights into candidates' abilities, problem-solving skills, and compatibility with the role and team.

Once you've selected the right candidates, successful induction is key to setting them up for success in their new roles. Providing a thorough orientation to the organization, team, and role helps new hires acclimate quickly and understand their responsibilities and expectations. This includes introducing them to key team members, providing access to necessary resources and training, and clarifying performance goals and objectives from the outset.

Understanding developmental needs is essential for fostering the growth and progression of your team members. Conducting training needs assessments can help you identify areas where employees require additional support or skill development. By investing in targeted training and development initiatives, such as workshops, courses, and mentorship programs, you can equip your team members with the knowledge and skills they need to excel in their roles and contribute to the team's success.

Various models and frameworks exist to guide the development of individuals within your team. These models may include approaches such as the GROW model (Goal, Reality, Options, Will), which provides a structured framework for coaching and development conversations, or competency-based development frameworks that outline the specific skills and behaviours required for success in different roles. By leveraging these models, managers can tailor development plans to meet the unique needs and goals of each team member, driving continuous improvement and professional growth.

In conclusion, selecting and developing the right people is a fundamental aspect of effective team formation and management. By honing your recruiting skills, providing successful induction, understanding developmental needs, and leveraging various models and tools for skill development, you can build a high-performing team capable of achieving its goals and driving organizational success. Investing in your team members' growth and development not only strengthens the team but also fosters a culture of continuous learning and improvement within the organization.

sYou can improve your recruiting skills with Hiring People – Questions to Ask, Inbox Assessment, Using Recruitment Tests, and Aptitude Testing. And you can develop people's skills with Successful

Induction, Understanding Developmental Needs, Training Needs Assessment, and various models.

Delegating Effectively

Having the right people with the right skills isn't sufficient for a team's success. Managers must also know how to get the job done efficiently. Delegation is the key to this. Some managers, especially those who earned their positions based on their technical expertise, try to do most of the work themselves. They think that, because they're responsible for the work, they should do it by themselves to make sure it's done right.

Delegating effectively is a fundamental skill for managers to maximize productivity and leverage the talents of their team members. While some managers may be inclined to handle tasks themselves, effective delegation involves assigning work to the right people and clearly outlining expectations to ensure that teams can accomplish more efficiently.

Managers who earned their positions based on technical expertise may initially struggle with delegation, feeling that they need to oversee every task to ensure it's done correctly. However, effective managers understand that by entrusting tasks to capable team members, they can leverage the diverse skills and capabilities of their team to achieve better results. Delegating tasks to the right people, rather than solely based on availability, is key to ensuring that projects are completed effectively and efficiently.

Building trust in the delegation process is essential for managers. Trusting team members to carry out tasks requires confidence in their skills, training, and motivation. Providing clear instructions, setting expectations, and offering support and resources as needed can help alleviate concerns and build confidence in team members' abilities to deliver results. Effective communication throughout the delegation process is crucial for clarifying objectives, timelines, and any potential challenges or obstacles.

Additionally, managers must resist the temptation to micromanage once tasks have been delegated. Micromanagement can stifle creativity, undermine trust, and hinder team members' growth and development. Instead, managers should empower team members to take ownership of their work and make decisions independently, while providing guidance and support as needed. Regular check-ins and progress updates can help managers stay informed without micromanaging, allowing team members to work autonomously while still feeling supported.

Ultimately, effective delegation involves trusting in the capabilities of your team members, providing clear direction and support, and empowering them to take ownership of their work. By delegating tasks effectively, managers can maximize productivity, foster a sense of ownership and accountability among team members, and achieve better results collectively. Embracing delegation as a strategic tool for leveraging the strengths of the team can lead to greater efficiency, innovation, and overall success for the organization.

Effective managers recognize that by assigning work to the right people (not just those with the most time available), and clearly outlining expectations, teams can accomplish much more. But it's often difficult to trust others to do the job. As a manager, remember that when your team members have the right skills, training and motivation, you can usually trust them to get the work done right.

Motivating People

Another necessary management skill is motivating others. It is one thing to motivate yourself, but it is quite another to motivate someone else. The key thing to remember is that motivation is personal. We're all motivated by different things, and we all have different levels of personal motivation.

Motivating others is a critical skill for managers to inspire and energize their teams. While motivating oneself may come naturally, motivating others requires a nuanced understanding of individual preferences, values, and drivers. Recognizing that motivation is personal and varies from person to person, effective managers invest time in getting to know their team members on a personal level to better understand what inspires and drives them.

Understanding what motivates each team member allows managers to tailor their approach to meet individual needs and preferences. Some employees may be driven by recognition and praise, while others may value opportunities for growth and development. By taking the time to understand these preferences, managers can provide personalized incentives and rewards that resonate with each team member, fostering a sense of engagement and commitment.

Providing regular feedback is a powerful strategy for keeping employees motivated and engaged. Feedback allows managers to acknowledge accomplishments, provide constructive criticism, and offer guidance for improvement. By offering timely and specific feedback, managers demonstrate their investment in the success and development of their team members, helping to build trust and confidence in their abilities.

In addition to individualized feedback, creating a positive work environment is essential for maintaining motivation. This involves fostering a culture of collaboration, respect, and recognition, where team members feel valued and appreciated for their contributions. Celebrating successes, promoting teamwork, and acknowledging milestones can help create a sense of camaraderie and motivation among team members.

Moreover, managers can encourage intrinsic motivation by providing meaningful work and opportunities for autonomy, mastery, and purpose. Empowering employees to take ownership of their work, develop new skills, and contribute to meaningful projects can increase their sense of fulfilment and engagement. Additionally, setting clear goals and expectations helps employees understand how their work contributes to the overall success of the team and organization, providing a sense of purpose and direction.

Overall, motivating others requires empathy, communication, and a genuine interest in understanding and supporting individual needs and aspirations. By building strong relationships, providing regular feedback, fostering a positive work environment, and promoting intrinsic motivation, managers can inspire their teams to achieve their goals and perform at their best. By recognizing and celebrating the unique talents and contributions of each team member, managers can cultivate a culture of motivation, engagement, and success within their organization.

So, getting to know your team members on a personal level allows you to motivate your people better. Providing feedback on a regular basis is a very powerful strategy to help you stay informed about what's happening with individual team members.

1. Managing Discipline and Dealing with Conflict

Sometimes, despite your best efforts, there are problems with individual performance. As a manager, you have to deal with these promptly. If you don't discipline, you risk negative impacts on the rest of the team as well as your customers, as poor performance typically impacts customer service, and it hurts the team and everything that the team has accomplished. It's very demotivating to work beside someone who consistently fails to meet expectations, so if you tolerate it, the rest of the team will likely suffer.

Managing discipline and addressing conflicts are inevitable challenges for managers, requiring prompt and effective action to maintain team performance and cohesion. When individual performance issues arise, managers must address them promptly to prevent negative impacts on the team and customer service. Failing to address poor performance not only undermines team morale but also jeopardizes the team's accomplishments and reputation.

Discipline is essential for upholding standards of performance and behavior within the team. When addressing performance issues, managers must communicate expectations clearly and provide constructive feedback to help employees understand where they are falling short. This may involve implementing performance improvement plans, setting specific goals and targets, and providing additional support and resources as needed. By addressing performance issues promptly and consistently, managers can demonstrate their commitment to maintaining a high-performance culture and holding team members accountable for their actions.

Conflict resolution is another critical aspect of managing discipline and maintaining team harmony. Conflict can arise from differences in opinion, communication styles, or competing priorities among team members. As a manager, it's important to address conflicts promptly and constructively, creating a safe space for open communication and collaboration. Utilizing a structured approach to conflict resolution, such as the three-step process outlined in our article on Resolving Team Conflict, can help managers facilitate productive discussions and find mutually acceptable solutions.

Moreover, managers must recognize that conflict can sometimes be positive, as it may highlight underlying structural problems within the team or organization. Rather than suppressing conflict or avoiding it altogether, managers should address its root causes to promote lasting resolution and prevent future issues from arising. This may involve examining team dynamics, communication processes, or organizational policies to identify areas for improvement and implement changes as needed.

Ultimately, effective management of discipline and conflict requires clear communication, empathy, and a willingness to address issues promptly and constructively. By setting clear expectations, providing support and guidance, and facilitating open dialogue among team members, managers can foster a positive work environment where conflicts are addressed proactively, and performance issues are resolved effectively. By managing discipline and conflict in a proactive and constructive manner, managers can uphold team morale, maintain productivity, and ensure the long-term success of the team and organization.

Team performance will also suffer when differences between individual team members turn into outright conflict, and it's your job as team manager to facilitate a resolution. Read our article on Resolving Team Conflict for a three-step process for doing this. However, conflict can be positive when it highlights underlying structural problems – make sure that you recognize conflict and deal with its causes, rather than just suppressing its symptoms or avoiding it.

2. Communicating

An element that's common to all of these management skills is effective communication. This is critical to any position you hold, but being a manager it is especially important. You need to let your team know what's happening and keep them informed as much as possible. Team briefing is a specific communication skill that managers should improve. Also, develop the ability to facilitate effectively, so that you can guide your team to a better understanding and serve as a moderator when necessary.

Effective communication is a cornerstone of successful management and is essential for fostering collaboration, clarity, and alignment within the team. As a manager, you play a pivotal role in keeping your team informed, engaged, and motivated, making effective communication a top priority in your role.

Keeping your team informed about important developments, changes, and expectations is crucial for maintaining transparency and trust. Regular team briefings provide an opportunity to share updates, discuss priorities, and address any questions or concerns. By keeping communication channels open and ensuring that information flows freely within the team, managers can empower team members to make informed decisions and contribute effectively to achieving shared goals.

Facilitating effective communication within the team is another key skill for managers. Facilitation involves guiding discussions, fostering collaboration, and ensuring that everyone has a voice and feels heard. By creating a supportive and inclusive environment where team members feel comfortable expressing their ideas and opinions, managers can harness the collective intelligence and creativity of the team. Effective facilitation also involves active listening, summarizing key points, and redirecting discussions as needed to keep conversations focused and productive.

Additionally, managers must be prepared to serve as moderators when conflicts or disagreements arise within the team. This requires the ability to remain impartial, listen to different perspectives, and guide the conversation towards a resolution. By facilitating constructive dialogue and helping team members find common ground, managers can prevent conflicts from escalating and promote positive relationships and collaboration within the team.

Furthermore, mastering written communication skills is essential for managers to convey information clearly and effectively. Whether its crafting emails, reports, or presentations, managers must communicate their messages in a concise, organized, and professional manner. Clarity, brevity, and empathy are key principles of effective written communication, ensuring that messages are understood and well-received by the intended audience.

In conclusion, effective communication is a critical skill for managers to master, encompassing both verbal and written communication, as well as facilitation and moderation abilities. By keeping your team informed, facilitating productive discussions, and serving as a moderator when conflicts arise, managers can create a positive and collaborative work environment where everyone feels valued and empowered to contribute. By prioritizing effective communication, managers can strengthen team cohesion, drive performance, and achieve organizational success.

3. Planning, Problem Solving and Decision-Making

Many managers are very comfortable with planning, problem solving and decision making, given that they're often skilled specialists who've been promoted because of their knowledge and analytical abilities. As such, one of the most important issues that managers experience is that they focus *so intensely* on these skills when they think about self-development that they fail to develop their people skills and team management skills. Make sure that you *don't* focus on these skills too much.

While planning, problem-solving, and decision-making are undoubtedly crucial skills for managers, it's essential not to overlook the development of people skills and team management abilities. Many managers excel in these analytical areas, often being promoted based on their technical expertise and knowledge. However, becoming too fixated on these skills can lead to neglecting the equally important aspects of managing and leading a team effectively.

Managers who prioritize planning, problem-solving, and decision-making may become overly focused on tasks and processes, neglecting the interpersonal dynamics and human element of leadership. Effective management requires a balance between technical proficiency and people skills, as managers must navigate complex relationships, inspire their teams, and foster a collaborative and supportive work environment.

Developing people skills involves cultivating empathy, communication, and emotional intelligence to understand and connect with team members on a personal level. Building strong relationships based on trust, respect, and mutual understanding is essential for fostering loyalty, engagement, and commitment among team members. Effective managers prioritize active listening, providing feedback, and recognizing individual contributions to create a positive and inclusive work culture where everyone feels valued and supported.

Similarly, mastering team management skills involves understanding team dynamics, facilitating collaboration, and resolving conflicts to ensure that teams perform at their best. Managers must create a clear vision and direction for the team, set achievable goals, and empower team members to take ownership of their work. Effective team management requires effective communication, delegation, and coaching to develop team members' skills and maximize their potential.

Furthermore, successful managers recognize the importance of continuous learning and self-development in both technical and interpersonal areas. By seeking opportunities for growth and improvement, managers can expand their skill set, deepen their understanding of leadership principles, and enhance their effectiveness as leaders.

In conclusion, while planning, problem-solving, and decision-making are essential skills for managers, it's equally important to develop people skills and team management abilities. Effective management requires a balance between technical proficiency and interpersonal competence, as managers must inspire, empower, and support their teams to achieve success. By prioritizing the development of both technical and interpersonal skills, managers can become more effective leaders and create a positive and high-performing work environment.

4. Avoiding Common Managerial Mistakes

Good communication helps you develop facilitation skills, and it also helps you avoid some of the most common problems for managers. Some of these common mistakes are thinking that you can rely on your technical skills alone, asking your boss to solve your problems, putting your boss in the awkward position of having to defend you, and not keeping your boss informed.

Avoiding common managerial mistakes is essential for maintaining credibility, effectiveness, and positive relationships within the organization. While technical skills are undoubtedly important, relying solely on them can lead to overlooking critical aspects of leadership and management. Effective communication is key to avoiding these common pitfalls and building strong relationships with both team members and superiors.

One common mistake is assuming that technical skills alone are sufficient for success in a managerial role. While technical expertise may have contributed to a manager's promotion, effective management requires a diverse skill set that encompasses communication, decision-making, problem-solving, and interpersonal skills. Managers must recognize the importance of continuous learning and development to enhance their leadership capabilities and adapt to evolving challenges and opportunities.

Additionally, relying on superiors to solve problems or defend decisions can undermine a manager's authority and autonomy. Effective managers take ownership of their responsibilities and seek solutions independently, demonstrating confidence and initiative in their decision-making. Building trust and credibility with superiors involves keeping them informed of important developments, seeking guidance when necessary, and proactively addressing challenges before they escalate.

Furthermore, effective communication is essential for maintaining open and transparent relationships with superiors. Managers must keep their superiors informed of project updates, challenges, and successes, providing regular updates and seeking feedback as needed. By fostering a culture of transparency and accountability, managers can build trust and credibility with their superiors and mitigate the risk of misunderstandings or miscommunications.

Avoiding common managerial mistakes requires a proactive approach to communication, decision-making, and relationship-building. Effective managers recognize the importance of balancing technical skills with interpersonal competence and take ownership of their responsibilities. By communicating openly, seeking solutions independently, and keeping superiors informed, managers can avoid common pitfalls and build strong, mutually beneficial relationships within the organization.

CHAPTER 2

The Power of Music

IT'S IMPACT ON THE INTELLECTUAL, SOCIAL AND PERSONAL DEVELOPMENT OF CHILDREN AND YOUNG PEOPLE

RECENT ADVANCES IN the study of the brain have enhanced our understanding of the way that active engagement with music may influence other activities. The cerebral cortex self-organizes as we engage with different musical activities; skills in these areas may then transfer to other activities if the processes involved are similar. Some skills transfer automatically without our conscious awareness; others require reflection on how they might be utilized in a new situation.

The power of music extends far beyond its auditory enjoyment; it has a profound impact on the intellectual, social, and personal development of children and young people. Recent advancements in neuroscience have shed light on the intricate relationship between music engagement and cognitive function, revealing how active involvement with music can influence various aspects of development.

One of the key findings in neuroscience is the concept of neuroplasticity, which refers to the brain's ability to reorganize and adapt in response to experiences and stimuli. Active engagement with music triggers neuroplasticity changes in the cerebral cortex, the outer layer of the brain responsible for higher cognitive functions. As individuals participate in musical activities such as playing instruments, singing, or listening attentively, neural connections are strengthened and refined, leading to improvements in auditory processing, memory, and executive function.

Moreover, the skills developed through music engagement have been found to transfer to other domains of learning and performance.

This phenomenon, known as transfer of learning, occurs when skills learned in one context are applied to another context with similar underlying processes. For example, the cognitive demands of learning to play a musical instrument, such as pattern recognition, attentional control, and motor coordination, can enhance academic achievement, problem-solving skills, and social competence.

Furthermore, music has a unique ability to foster social connections and emotional expression, enriching interpersonal relationships and promoting empathy and cooperation. Collaborative musical activities, such as ensemble performance or group singing, encourage communication, teamwork, and mutual support among participants. Additionally, music serves as a universal language that transcends cultural and linguistic barriers, allowing individuals to connect and communicate on a deeper level.

On a personal level, music has a profound impact on emotional well-being and self-expression. Listening to music can evoke a wide range of emotions, from joy and excitement to introspection and contemplation, providing an outlet for emotional release and stress relief. Moreover, active engagement with music, such as song writing or improvisation, allows individuals to express their thoughts, feelings, and experiences creatively, fostering self-awareness and identity development.

The power of music to influence intellectual, social, and personal development is undeniable. Through its effects on neuroplasticity, transfer of learning, social interaction, and emotional expression, music enriches the lives of children and young people in profound and meaningful ways. By promoting active engagement with music in educational and community settings, we can nurture the holistic development of individuals and empower them to reach their full potential.

Perceptual, language and literacy skills

Speech and music have a number of shared processing systems. Musical experiences which enhance processing can therefore impact on the perception of language which in turn impacts on learning to read.

Active engagement with music sharpens the brain's early encoding of linguistic sound. Eight year old children with just 8 weeks of musical training showed improvement in perceptual cognition compared with controls.

Speech makes extensive use of structural auditory patterns based on timbre differences between phonemes. Musical training develops skills which enhance perception of these patterns. This is critical in developing phonological awareness which in turn contributes to learning to read successfully.

Speech processing requires similar processing to melodic contour. Eight year old children with musical training outperformed controls on tests of music and language.

Learning to discriminate differences between tonal and rhythmic patterns and to associate these with visual symbols seems to transfer to improved phonemic awareness.

Learning to play an instrument enhances the ability to remember words through enlargement of the left cranial temporal regions. Musically trained participants remembered more verbal information that those without musical training.

Children experiencing difficulties with reading comprehension have benefitted from training in rhythmical performance. Research exploring the relationships between mathematics and active musical engagement has had mixed results, in part, because not all mathematics' tasks share underlying processes with those involved in music. Transfer is dependent on the extent of the match, for instance, children receiving instruction on rhythm instruments scored higher on part-whole math's problems than those receiving piano and singing instruction.

Intellectual development

Learning an instrument has an impact on intellectual development, particularly spatial reasoning. Contrasting the impact of music lessons (standard keyboard, Kodaly voice) with drama or no lessons found that the music groups had reliably larger increases in I.Q.

A key issue arising is what kinds of musical activity bring about change in particular kinds of intellectual development and why. Some offering a broad musical education, others focused more closely on instrumental tuition. To begin to address these questions, active engagement with making music can have an impact on intellectual development. What requires further is to research in the specific types of musical participation which develop skills which transfer automatically to other areas and what are the common features of these skills.

General attainment and creativity

There is a consistent relationship between active engagement in music and general attainment but much research has been unable to partial out confounding factors. It needs further study, adopting more sensitive statistical modeling to overcome these difficulties. However music participation enhances measured creativity, particularly when the musical activity itself is creative, for instance, improvisation.

Personal and social development

General attainment may be influenced by the impact that music has on personal and social development. Playing an instrument can lead to a sense of achievement; an increase in self-esteem; increased confidence; persistence in overcoming frustrations when learning is difficult; self-discipline; and provide a means of self-expression. These may increase motivation for learning in general thus supporting enhanced attainment.

Participating in musical groups promotes friendships with like-minded people; self-confidence; social skills; social networking; a sense of belonging; team work; self-discipline; a sense of accomplishment; co-operation; responsibility; commitment; mutual support; bonding to meet group goals; increased concentration and provides an outlet for relaxation.

Working in small musical groups requires the development of trust and respect and skills of negotiation and compromise.

In adolescence music makes a major contribution to the development of self-identity and is seen as a source of support when young people are feeling troubled or lonely. Music has been linked to the capacity to increase emotional sensitivity. The recognition of emotions in music is related to emotional intelligence.

Increasing the amount of classroom music within the curriculum can increase social cohesion within class, greater self-reliance, better social adjustment and more positive attitudes, particularly in low ability, disaffected pupils.

The positive effects of engagement with music on personal and social development will only occur if, overall, it is an enjoyable and rewarding experience. The quality of the teaching, the extent to which individuals perceive that they are successful, and whether in the long term it is a positive experience will all contribute to the nature of any personal or social benefits.

Physical development, health and wellbeing

Rhythmic accompaniment to physical education enhances the development of physical skills. Learning to play an instrument enhances fine motor co-ordination. There may be particular health benefits for singing in relation to the immune system, breathing, adopting good posture, improved mood, and stress reduction. The research has been carried out with adults but these benefits could equally apply to children.

Effect of Music Lessons on the Intelligence Quotient (I.Q.)

One of the first ability that is enhanced by music is creativity. Studies on children have shown that they paint more creatively, if they are simultaneously listening to music. The visual and space orientation capacities have been shown to improve for a short while (10-15 minutes), after listening to music; this is a part of the Mozart effect. It is believed that intelligence levels are increased by listening Mozart's compositions, hence the name particular name of this effect.

However, from merely listening to further studying music, the latter step is considerably important, and consequently the results can be observed. Simple listening differs significantly from the actual learning process of playing an instrument or singing. In the process of learning music, the brain modifies and actually enlarges within certain areas that are connected with this particular task.

The effect of music lessons on Intelligence Quotient (IQ) has been a topic of interest and debate among researchers and educators for decades. While the relationship between music education and cognitive development is complex and multifaceted, numerous studies have explored the potential impact of music lessons on IQ and related cognitive abilities.

One of the key theories underlying the connection between music education and IQ is the concept of neuroplasticity, which refers to the brain's ability to reorganize and adapt in response to experiences and stimuli. Music education involves active engagement with auditory, motor, and cognitive processes, leading to neuroplasticity changes in the brain's structure and function. As individuals learn to play instruments, read music notation, and interpret musical patterns, neural connections are strengthened and refined, enhancing various aspects of cognitive function.

Several studies have investigated the relationship between music education and IQ, with mixed findings. Some research suggests that music lessons may have a positive impact on IQ scores, particularly in domains such as spatial reasoning, mathematical ability, and verbal memory. For example, a longitudinal study conducted by Schellenberg (2004) found that children who received keyboard or voice lessons over a period of one year showed greater improvements in IQ compared to those who received drama or no extracurricular lessons. Similarly, a meta-analysis by Sala and Gobet (2017) found a small but significant positive effect of music training on IQ scores in children and adolescents.

However, it is essential to note that the relationship between music education and IQ is not straightforward, and the magnitude of the effect may vary depending on factors such as the duration and intensity of music instruction, the age of the participants, and individual differences in cognitive abilities. Furthermore, some studies have failed to find a significant relationship between music lessons and IQ, suggesting that other factors may also play a role in cognitive development.

One possible explanation for the mixed findings is that the effects of music education on IQ are mediated by other factors, such as motivation, self-discipline, and parental involvement. Engaging in music lessons requires sustained effort, practice, and perseverance, which may foster the development of important cognitive and non-cognitive skills that contribute to overall intelligence. Additionally, the social and emotional benefits of music education, such as increased self-esteem, confidence, and social connectedness, may indirectly influence cognitive functioning and academic achievement.

Moreover, the specific components of music education, such as instrumental versus vocal training, individual versus group instruction, and the integration of music theory and improvisation, may also influence the cognitive outcomes. For example, research suggests that learning to play a musical instrument may have differential effects on cognitive abilities compared to passive listening or singing. Similarly, engaging in collaborative music-making activities, such as ensemble performance or composition, may enhance social cognition and interpersonal skills in addition to cognitive function.

While the relationship between music education and IQ is complex and multifaceted, there is evidence to suggest that music lessons may have a positive impact on cognitive development in children and adolescents. However, the magnitude and specificity of the effect may vary depending on various factors, including the duration and intensity of music instruction, individual differences in cognitive abilities, and the specific components of music education. Further research is needed to elucidate the underlying mechanisms and determine the optimal conditions for maximizing the cognitive benefits of music education.

Several studies (Pascual-Leone, 2001) and brain scans have revealed that the musicians' brain is different; for example a piano player has got more gray matter in the region that controls the finger movements. In the study named "The Effects of Musical Training on Structural Brain Development", several scientists namely Krista L. Hyde, Alan C. Evans (from Montreal Neurological Institute, McGill University), Jason Lerch (Mouse Imaging Centre, Hospital for Sick Children, Toronto, Ontario, Canada), Gottfried Schlaug, Andrea Norton, Marie Forgeard (from the Department of Neurology, Music and Neuroimaging Laboratory, Beth Israel Deaconess (Medical Center and Harvard Medical School), and Ellen Winner (from the Department of Psychology, Boston College, Chestnut Hill, Massachusetts, USA), have brought relevant insight regarding how music really helps to develop our brain, and successively our IQ. They investigated the structural changes that occur in the brain as a result of 15 months of instrumental music teaching program that was conducted for young children; they were compared with another group of children that did not have any musical training. As expected, the former group showed improved finger movement and rhythm related tasks. However, the tasks that did not involve musical knowledge remained the same. The gray matter development has also been observed in areas other than those directly connected with music, namely, hearing and finger movement. The complex process of learning produces growth in other parts of the brain, and these facts lead to the idea that long-term programs of brain training may help neuron growth in children. This is particularly relevant for those with developmental problems, as well as for grownups with neurological conditions.

Musicians generally have more gray matter as compared to non-musicians, and also have a significant increase in the gray matter quantity. When professional and amateur musicians are compared, it is clearly revealed that the former type who actually practice twice as much have a greater brain development, than the amateurs. Studies conducted on musicians and non-musicians explain a diversity of differences, some notable and some statistically proven. Also, increased memory levels have been noticed in musically trained children within ages of 4 - 6, when compared to the non-musical children of the same age. The list of tasks where it has been observed that musically trained people perform better is: vocabulary, math, reading, verbal memory, space orientation skills, and phonemic awareness.

Another study by E. Glenn Schellenberg (2006) shows that musically trained school children got better results on IQ tests. Several intellectual abilities are connected to music learning, and seem to have a beneficial influence in developing musicians' memory in areas that are connected to fluid intelligence like the speed of processing, verbal comprehension, working memory, and perceptual organization.

This overview provides a strong case for the benefits of active engagement with music throughout the lifespan. In early childhood there seem to be benefits for the development of perceptual skills which effect learning language subsequently impacting on literacy which is also enhanced by opportunities to develop rhythmic co-ordination. Fine motor co-ordination is improved through learning to play an instrument. Music also seems to improve spatial reasoning, one aspect of general intelligence which is related to some of the skills required in mathematics. While general attainment is clearly affected by literacy and numeracy skills, motivation which depends on self-esteem, self-efficacy and aspirations is also important in the amount of effort given to studying. Engagement with music can enhance self-perceptions but only if it provides positive learning experiences which are rewarding. This means that musical experiences need to be enjoyable providing challenges which are also attainable. Teaching needs to generate an environment which is supportive and sufficiently flexible to facilitate the development of creativity and self-expression. Group music making is also beneficial to the development of social skills and can contribute to health and well-being throughout the lifespan and can therefore contribute to community cohesion providing benefits to society as a whole.

Effect of Classical Music on Babies

Music can be an extremely powerful stimulant. It can completely sway our emotions. A soft, gentle song can make you hum in delight, a song about overcoming difficulties can make you optimistic and give you the strength to carry on, a soothing sound can help you sleep, and an energetic orchestra can make you feel excitement. There have been several studies done on the effect that music can have on our mind.

Some of these studies have predominantly focused on how music can affect the minds of babies. It is believed that music can actually affect the way our mind functions, especially in our developmental years. It is believed that music can have an influence on one's mood and language skills. The importance of music is a matter that has been studied widely, and its effect on one's mood and minds has been widely accepted. This effect is not restricted to only infants but can also be seen in adults.

According to scientists, listening to classical music during your infancy will not make you smarter but it does have an effect on the passages that are built in the brain to facilitate the functioning of neurons. It is a well-known fact that with age the number of neurons that we use depletes and the exposing babies to stimuli like music that is considered classical can improve the functioning of neurons which results in ready acceptance of knowledge and talent. Have you ever been shocked at news reports of child prodigies who can play symphonies by Mozart and Beethoven at the age of three? Well, chances are that these kids were exposed to classical music as infants. Not only do they remember these pieces of music, but they also retain the ability to process and remember any other information they were exposed to while listening to classical music.

Studies have also shown that classical music can actually improve your spatial abilities and aid your language learning skills. Research has shown that babies who were exposed to classical music tend to have much higher spatial IQs compared to babies who were not made to listen to classical music. Also their ability to understand language and learn it was much better, as listening to classical music helped them understand and differentiate between complex sounds. As with adults the mood of a baby can also be greatly affected by the music that is playing in the background. Classical music can have a huge effect on a baby's health. It has been observed that listening to classical music can help calm the mind of an infant and also alleviate pain, especially in babies who are born premature.

If you are a new parent who wants to ensure that your baby benefits a lot, then you can introduce your child to classical music at an early age by playing music for them. Ensure though that you control the volume levels of the music. Several parents also choose to sing to their kids who can often help them not only understand and recognize your voice but also help them develop their language skills. While definitely not harmful for your child, it should be seen as a learning aid and nothing more than that.

The effect of classical music on babies has been a subject of interest and inquiry among parents, researchers, and healthcare professionals for many years. The notion that exposing infants to classical music can have positive effects on their development has gained widespread attention, fuelled in part by popular media and marketing campaigns promoting the concept of the "Mozart effect." While the scientific evidence supporting specific cognitive benefits of classical music for babies is mixed and often debated, there is growing recognition of the potential influence of music exposure on various aspects of infant development, including auditory perception, emotional regulation, and social bonding.

One of the primary reasons parents may introduce classical music to their babies is the belief that it can enhance cognitive abilities, such as intelligence and problem-solving skills. This idea stems from the work of psychologist Frances Rauscher and her colleagues, who reported in a seminal study published in 1993 that college students who listened to Mozart's Sonata for Two Pianos in D major showed temporary improvements in spatial reasoning tasks. While subsequent research has failed to replicate these findings consistently, the concept of the "Mozart effect" captured the public imagination and led to a surge in interest in the potential cognitive benefits of classical music for people of all ages, including infants.

In addition to its purported cognitive effects, classical music is often praised for its soothing and calming qualities, making it a popular choice for creating a peaceful environment for babies. The slow tempo, gentle melodies, and harmonious compositions of classical music have been shown to reduce stress and promote relaxation in both infants and adults. Playing classical music during bedtime or naptime routines may help babies unwind and transition to sleep more easily, contributing to improved sleep quality and overall well-being.

Furthermore, exposure to classical music during infancy may play a role in shaping auditory perception and language development.

The intricate patterns, varied rhythms, and rich tonalities of classical compositions provide a rich auditory experience for babies, stimulating their auditory senses and laying the groundwork for language acquisition. Research suggests that infants are sensitive to the musical elements of rhythm, pitch, and timbre from a very young age and may respond positively to classical music stimuli. Additionally, listening to music with repetitive patterns and predictable structures may help infants develop auditory discrimination skills and enhance their ability to detect subtle sound differences, which are essential for language processing and communication.

Beyond its cognitive and auditory effects, classical music has the power to evoke emotional responses and facilitate social bonding between babies and caregivers. Music has been described as a universal language that transcends cultural and linguistic barriers, communicating emotions and feelings in ways that words alone cannot. Sharing musical experiences with babies, such as singing lullabies or playing classical music together, can create opportunities for emotional connection, attunement, and mutual enjoyment between parents and infants. Music has been shown to activate brain regions associated with emotion processing and social bonding, fostering feelings of warmth, security, and attachment in both infants and adults.

However, it is essential to recognize that the effects of classical music on babies are complex and multifaceted, and individual responses may vary. While some babies may show a preference for classical music and exhibit signs of enjoyment or relaxation when exposed to it, others may be indifferent or even distressed by certain musical stimuli. Additionally, the quality and context of music exposure, as well as individual differences in temperament and sensory processing, may influence the observed effects.

While the scientific evidence supporting specific cognitive benefits of classical music for babies may be inconclusive, there is growing recognition of the potential influence of music exposure on various aspects of infant development, including auditory perception, emotional regulation, and social bonding. Parents may choose to introduce classical music to their babies as a means of creating a soothing environment, stimulating cognitive development, and fostering emotional connection and social interaction. However, it is essential to approach music exposure with sensitivity and awareness of individual differences, and to prioritize the emotional well-being and comfort of the baby above all else.

The 'Brain' and the 'Mind'

As we all know that the **brain** is an organ of soft nervous tissue contained in the skull of vertebrates, functioning as the coordinating center of sensation and intellectual and nervous activity. It also indicates the intellectual capacity which may synonymy as intelligence, mental capacity, brain power, cleverness, powers of reasoning, sagacity, judgment, common sense etc.

The brain is the control center for all the body's functions, such as walking, talking, swallowing, breathing, taste, smell, heart rate and so on. It also controls all our thinking functions, our emotions, how we behave and all our intellectual (cognitive) activities, such as how we attend to things, how we perceive and understand our world and its physical surroundings, how we learn and remember and so on.

Damage to a particular part of the brain can produce impairment in the function that it controls. If the damage is limited to a small area, then it is likely that only a few functions will be impaired. If, however, as is more common, there is widespread damage, then this can produce a complex array of physical and psychological problems. The level of impairment will depend on the type, location and severity of the injury.

When thinking of cognitive problems, it is useful to remember that no human skills operate in isolation. We depend on a combination of several skills to carry out individual tasks. For example, if we want to remember what someone is saying to us, we firstly have to be able to:

- Attend to what they are saying (concentration)
- Understand what they are saying (language/information-processing)
- Keep up with the flow of conversation (speed of thought)

Similarly, a loss of one skill can affect another skill. For example, a memory problem can actually be the result of an attention problem. For this reason, it is important for the Acquired Brain Injury (ABI) survivor to have a neuro-psychological assessment, which will identify more precisely the areas of difficulty. Most people who have suffered a brain injury will experience some cognitive difficulties, to a lesser or greater extent, particularly in the early stages of recovery. However, while there may be marked improvements in cognitive skills over time, some degree of permanent disability is common for people who have suffered a severe brain injury. The most common complaints, for which strategies have been listed here, are concentration, speed of processing information and memory.

Emotional and behavioral changes can reflect a fundamental change in personality for some ABI survivors while for others they may represent an exaggeration of a previous personality. The changes that occur reflect a combination of physical damage to the emotional control centers of the brain and the psychological reaction to the injury and its effects.

How an individual copes emotionally will depend to a large extent on their previous personality, level of insight and the amount of family and professional support made available to them. Again, it is important to remember that different people will experience different levels of changes.

Mind is the element of a person that enables them to be aware of the world and their experiences, to think, and to feel; the faculty of consciousness and thought. In other words it is a person's ability to think and reason; the intellect.

The mind is basically a communication and control system between the theta - the spiritual being that is the person himself - and his environment. It is composed of mental image pictures which are recordings of past experiences. The individual uses his mind to pose and solve problems related to survival and to direct his efforts according to these solutions.

The mind is made up of two parts - the analytical mind and the reactive mind. The analytical mind is the rational, conscious, aware mind which thinks, observes data, remembers it and resolves problems. The sentient portion of the mind - the actual computing ability of

Man - is never in error. Yet if the mind always computes perfectly on the data that it has stored and perceived, how is it then that people make errors in judgment? Just as with a machine that has a held down "7" button, when incorrect data gets fed into the human memory banks, it can cause a person to make errors and act in an abnormal manner.

The reactive mind is the portion of a person's mind which works on a totally stimulus-response basis. It is not under volitional control, and exerts force and the power of command over awareness, purposes, thoughts, body and actions. Hypnosis, which has nothing to do with Dianetic therapy (a method for curing mental disorder by releasing engrams. This therapy is administered by an "auditor" who effects the release, freeing the patient from the deleterious influence of engrams) nevertheless serves as a laboratory tool to demonstrate how that portion of the mind that is not in contact with the consciousness still acts upon an individual. This is called the "Reactive Mind," and is the source of insanity, psychosomatic ills and further aberrations.

Effects of Classical Music on the Brain

Listening to classical music becomes an addiction when you start feeling the lyrics and allow the melody to get infused in to your mind. A lot of research has been done on the effects that classical music has on the brain, and the results have been proven true. The effects are more pronounced when you submerge yourself completely into the music and listen to it religiously without diverting your mind anywhere else. The rhythms harmonize with the vibrations present inside your mind and you feel intensely relaxed. Classical music is capable of mellowing down your agitated mind and soothing your senses in a unique way. We explain you further in the upcoming segment. How Does Classical Music Affect the Brain the two significant elements of classical music that make it so intensely appealing, are its rhythm and melody. The rhythm acts like a stimulant for the brain while the melody sparks up your mind. Melody and rhythm when combined together affect the performance and organization of the brain in the positive direction.

Several studies have shown that production of serotonin is elevated in the brain when a person is engrossed in the music. It's a sleep inducing hormone that also acts as an antidepressant. Secretion of serotonin takes place when your brain is exposed to positive shock, like music, poetry, movies, etc. When your mind is tuned to the notes of classical music then you can automatically sense a pleasing aura around you. The soothing vibe that you feel around yourself is the outcome of serotonin which is released under the effect of classical music. Scientists also say that, classical music can bring down the levels of hormone cortisone, whose excessive presence can cause anxiety, stress and depression.

Instrumental classical music from India and other Eastern countries has a spellbinding effect on the brain. Classical music played with instruments, like *santoor, sarod, sitar* and flute can rejuvenate your mind instantly. The harmony in the notes and the soft melody played can improve your concentration power. You can resort to this form of music while suffering from anxiety, exhaustion and restlessness. Classical music also encourages your creative instincts, which is a direct outcome of the effects it has on your brain.

The most pronounced is the effect of Mozart's 60 beat per minute composition of the baroque period. The Mozart Effect says that, *improvement on the performance of spatiotemporal reasoning and short-term memory takes place through the listening of complex music, such as Mozart's two-piano concertos.* The waves generated inside the brain have a specific amplitude and frequency. Listening to this particular form of music can influence the pattern of the waves produced inside the brain. It further improves your reasoning and cognitive abilities. As a consequence of change in frequency and amplitude of the waves, your brain responds quickly and it is able to process information more swiftly. You can read the book, 'The Mozart Effect: Tapping the Power of Music to Heal the Body, Strengthen the Mind, and Unlock the Creative Spirit', written by Don Campbell for acquiring in depth knowledge about this phenomenon.

Exposing your child to classical music can also bring about significant changes in his brain. The IQ of your child is boosted up and his grasping power is also enhanced. An effect of classical music on babies has been reported with development of superior skills and talents. Infants brought up in an ambiance of different forms of classical music, like Beethoven's symphony, Mozart's piano or Hindustani classical music has higher spatial IQ. Considerable improvement in functioning of the neurons was observed that further sharpens their knowledge and intellect level. In short, the melody of classical music refines their ability to understand things.

I hope you have been delighted to know the positive effects of classical music on the brain. Make the intensely absorbing melody a part of your life and enjoy the bliss. Even expecting mothers can listen classical music once a day to rejuvenate their mind and keep themselves fresh and energetic.

Music can affect the brain in the following ways:

Increases Concentration Levels, Improves Memory: It is known that music helps increase your concentration levels. It helps improve memory. It has been found to increase memory levels of Alzheimer's and dementia patients. Research has shown that the silence between two musical notes triggers brain cells which are responsible for the development of sharp memory. Flute music, and instruments like *santoor* and *sarod* are recommended for the enhancement of concentration and memory. Classical music improves the ability to recall what's retained in the brain in the form of memory. Strong beats causes the brain waves to resonate in synch with the beat, thus leading to increased levels of concentration and increased mental alertness. This also trains the brain to change speeds of processing easily, as need be. Learning music helps increase self-discipline.

Increases Creativity and Problem-solving Skills: Music plays a vital role in enhancing creativity. Music has a positive impact on the right side of the brain. Music triggers brain centers which deal with the enhancement of creativity. Certain *ragas* are known to activate the *chakras* of our body, thus giving us an added advantage in other creative tasks. Music increases spatial and abstract reasoning skills. These are the skills required in tackling problems, solving puzzles and taking decisions. Listening to Mozart's music is known to have a positive effect on the spatial-temporal reasoning, simply put, it makes you smarter.

Makes Learning Easier: Have you tried learning anything by combining it with music or rhythm? For example, counting with a certain repeating pattern, or learning the alphabet by giving it a tune. Or remember learning poetry by reciting it musically? Didn't that help you learn things faster? Basically you can remember songs because they are musical compositions and not plain words lacking music or rhythm. This is what music does. It makes learning easier. Learning beat patterns (*talas*), helps improve math skills. The study of rhythm is known to help students learn math. Music stimulates the brain centers that deal with thinking, analyzing and planning, thus enhancing one's organizational skills.

Speeds Healing: Music helps in the secretion of endorphins that help in speeding the process of healing. It acts as an effective distraction from pain and suffering. It not only diverts the mind from pain, but also helps bring about certain chemical changes in the brain that help speed the healing process. Music therapy is recommended for patients of high blood pressure, heart diseases and even cancer. Music is therapeutic in pain management. Listening to melodious, comforting music is sure to have a positive effect on the physical and mental well-being of patients. If not cure every ailment, music definitely creates hope in the minds of patients - a hope to recover. And when nothing else works, only hope does.

Effects of Music on the Mind

The study of how music affects the mind has been a subject of interest for many. The interconnection between music and the physical and mental health of human beings has been researched on since long. Research has concluded that music does have positive effects on our mind. It has the power of healing certain ailments. Indian classical music has been found to have the strongest healing powers. Music has a calming effect on the mind. It is known to speed the recovery of health ailments. It helps fight anxiety and has a soothing effect on the brain.

Music effects on the mental state in the following ways:

***Fights Depression*:** Feeling depressed, gloomy or inadequate? Soothing music can help you. Depression reduces brain activity and hampers the mind's ability to plan and carry out tasks. Lack of the neurotransmitter, Serotonin, results in a depressed state of mind.

Soothing musical notes help increase the Serotonin levels of the brain, thus alleviating mental depression. Natural musical notes are known to make the mind alert.

***Relieves Anxiety*:** Anxiety is a feeling of fear or uncertainty that clouds your mind and the feeling is mostly about an upcoming event having an unknown outcome. The result is what you are afraid of or worried about. Increased anxiety levels and stress lead to sleeplessness. Prolonged periods of anxiety may even lead to anxiety disorders. But, music can come to rescue. It calms the body nerves and soothes the mind. Flat musical notes induce sleep.

***Improves Learning Abilities*:** Music affects the process of learning and thinking. Listening to quiet and soothing music while working helps you work faster and in a more efficient way. Music has the ability to make you positive and feel motivated. Research has shown that music brings about remarkable improvements in the academic skills of students, who are made to listen to certain kinds of music while studying or working in the lab. Listening to pleasant music, while doing a difficult task, can make it seem easier.

***Boosts Confidence*:** Music has a positive effect on the interpersonal skills of an individual. Lack of confidence and very less or no desire to learn is most often the reason behind a failure. It's not always inability. Students obtaining poor school grades do not necessarily lack intelligence. It's their disinterest in the subjects or the lack of motivation that leads to poor academic performance. Music lessons during school can help the students fight their mental block. Music proves helpful in encouraging young children to venture new fields. It increases their capacity to believe in themselves, that is, in boosting confidence.

How Music Affects Heart Rate

Most of us love music and some are even addicted to it; be it rock, pop, classical, jazz, etc. There is hardly anyone who doesn't listen to or enjoys any type of music. This is because music is known to have certain effects on us. Some of us claim that music elevates their mood, some say that it brings about a feeling of calmness or tranquility, or some may even say that it brings out the wild side in them. It is said that music strikes the chord of right emotions in our mind, or touches our heart. Studies undertaken to find the effect of music on human beings have found that this is not a myth anymore. Music definitely affects the heart, or the cardiovascular system. Let us know how.

Have you experienced a condition when listening to very loud music makes your heartbeat so fast that you can actually feel the heavy beating? In that case, you become anxious and restless. This is because of the effect loud music has on your heart rate. From this experience, it is concluded that loud and faster music increases the heart rate. Therefore, we have a feeling of high anxiety, hyperactivity, stress, etc. when we listen to music which has a faster tempo.

On the contrary, slower music or music that has a slower tempo is associated with a slower heart rate. People who listen to calming music or classical music have a slower heart rate as compared to those listening to fast paced music, or those not listening to music at all.

But, why does this happen? The music and heart rate experiment found that the effect of music on the heart is based on the functioning of the brain. When we hear music, the sound waves produced are translated into electrical impulses by the brain. These impulses are sent to the hypothalamus. As it is related to the increasing and decreasing of the heart rate, the related effect is produced. Now you may wonder, is it that only slow music brings out this effect? Well, listening to slow or calming music is definitely more beneficial. However, listening to any type of music you like can be helpful, rather than not listening to any music at all.

Now let us try to understand why a slower heart rate beneficial to human beings. Heart rate is nothing but the pulse rate, i.e., the number of times your heart beats per minute. It is believed that people who have a slower heart rate have a longer life. Similarly, people having a higher heart rate are at a greater risk of suffering from cardiovascular diseases. Therefore, having a slower heart rate is definitely more beneficial. When music slows down the heart rate, it brings about a feeling of calmness and hence, it is used as a relaxation technique. Music also helps in bringing about an overall feeling of wellness, besides it also helps in reducing stress and relieving anxiety. You should remember that listening to any kind of music (in right frequency and right tempo) is surely beneficial for the overall health. Lastly, we can conclude by saying that the phrase '*heals the heart*' in the following quote is not just a saying, but a fact! *Music speaks what cannot be expressed, soothes the mind and gives it rest, heals the heart and makes it whole, flows from heaven to the soul.*

How does Music affect your Mood?

Some look at music as a hobby; for some music is their passion, while some pursue music as their career. Music has a direct influence on your mood. Book stores, restaurants and shopping malls often keep some music playing in the background. The kind of music they choose to play depends on the kind of audiences they target. Music is found to enhance customer experience. Music in malls and restaurants peps up customers' mood. People tend to spend more time in the mall or hotel that plays pleasant music. Music brightens up the atmosphere around you and cheers you up. Music can make you cry, music can make you smile; it has a direct impact on your mood. How music affects your mood also depends on what you associate that piece of music with. A tune or a particular song that is in some way related to your childhood can bring back memories. A song you associate something or someone in your life with, can remind you of that person or thing.

Negative Effects that Music Can Have

For music to have positive effects on the mind and brain, it should be complex enough to involve brain activity. It should be synchronous and generate sound waves that are in tune with the body's internal rhythm. It should be played at a volume the listeners' ears can accept and should have regular beats to have any good effects on the body and mind rhythm and functioning. Here are some of the negative effects of music.

Very loud music can disturb the symmetry between the right and left halves of the brain. Loud music results in a disturbed state of mind. Exposure to harsh or disruptive music at an early age can lead to learning disabilities and behavior problems in children.

According to a study by Dr. John Diamond, an Australian physician and psychiatrist, body muscles go weak when subjected to the stopped anapestic beat in hard rock music. He also says that shrill frequencies and irregular beats are harmful to the mind and body. Disharmony in music has been shown to reduce retention levels of the brain and lead to aggression and hyperactivity. Heavily repeating musical patterns can lead to feelings of anger and boredom.

So, the effects music can have on your mind or brain depend largely on the kind of music you choose to listen to. To experience positive psychological effects of music, you should listen to only good music. A sound which spells melody is good music. It's the sound that has the power of creating calm. That's the magic of music, I think. Listening to music gives me divine pleasure. What about you?

How Music Affects Our Moods

Friedrich Nietzsche once said, *"Without music, life would be a mistake."* It is probably a sentiment that most of us would agree with without any form of challenge. Music is almost omnipresent, existing in infinite things around us. Every time you listen to a piece of music you are taken back to a memory, something that you associate with that particular lilting tune. Not only does music bring back memories, it can also at many levels affect how we feel. How many times have you listened to a beautifully sung sad ballad and felt tears streaming down your face? And how many times has a song with a cheerful tempo made you smile? Music has a power that not many other things do. Music can have a profound effect on your mood, and in this article, we will take a look at the effect of music on our moods.

The Effect of Music on One's Mood

Have you ever wondered as to why malls, restaurants, and even movie theater lobbies have music playing? Well, to understand this simply just look back at how you have felt when you have heard music play at these places. Music is known to enhance how a customer feels and playing the right type of music can help people feel better and also brighten the ambiance of the place. Often music also has an effect on your concentration and can help you increase your levels of focus. Music helps the secretion of endorphins thereby helping patients feel positive and help them heal faster and better.

Depression is a state of mind that most of us experience at some point of time or the other. There are periods in our life when everything can seem difficult and inadequate. It can seem like everything is going downhill and you have absolutely no control over your life. Studies have shown that music can be a major mood lifter in such situations. Music is known to help increase the levels of serotonin in your brain thus reducing depression.

Music also plays a great role in reducing anxiety. Anxiety can often cause lack of sleep and other related disorders. Listening to music can help calm the nerves and reduce the anxiety one is experiencing. The effects of music on the mind and brain are something that has been the subject of many studies.

Music is often known as the international language. We may not know the language another person is speaking but most of us respond to music in the same manner. If the tempo is upbeat, you will dance to the music, if it is slow, soulful number, you will sway it. Music can often be the best way to connect with someone. It is one of the best ways to enhance your moods, but this can depend a lot on the kind of music you listen to. While happy music can definitely make you feel better, sad music can further drown your spirits.

Listening to classical music can often make you feel a lot more powerful while soft lilting music can be the perfect way to unwind at the end of a long day. If you want to use music to change the way you are feeling, you need to understand how it affects you. Learn to recognize the kind of music that elevates your mood and helps you feel better. Once you are aware of the kind of music you can use, you can use it to change the way you feel. The right kind of music can be the perfect to way feel more euphoric. In order to allow music to affect your mood, you need to have the requisite faith that it will work.

At the most basic of levels, all music does is entertain us. If you look more closely though music revitalizes us, it thrills us, makes us feel powerful, is a distraction, can be a great way to make us more creative, and can help us connect with something we were unaware of or had forgotten. In the 2007 movie August Rush, the titular character says something about music that many of us identify with, *"Listen. Can you hear it? The music. I can hear it everywhere. In the wind... in the air... in the light. It's all around us. All you have to do is open yourself up. All you have to do... is to listen."* If you want to know how music affects our moods, all you need to do... is to feel.

CHAPTER 3

Classical Music and Its Elements

IT'S THE BEAUTIFUL arrangement and harmony in the components of classic music that spellbound its listeners so much. The period within 1750 - 1830 is known as the Classical period, during which musicians and singers like Wolfgang Amadeus Mozart, Johann Sebastian Bach, Franz Schubert and Ludwig van Beethoven created a history in classical music. The popularity of classical music had a far flung effect and even common people developed an inclination for it. Singers and composers experimented with different styles and practiced use of different types of instruments for creating new genres.

Singing classical songs is truly difficult if you are not well versed with its elements, forms and characteristics. The approach and concept of people about classical music although differ a lot, yet there are some traits that are common in all. Classical music elements actually refer to the parts, sections and the components of the music that make it complete. Such elements form an integral part of different types of musical instruments, like violin, saxophone, piano, guitar, percussion, flute, etc. The essence of classical music lies in harmonizing the notes and chords to generate a tune where we can submerge ourselves completely. It's because these elements are blended so well, classical music is capable of rejuvenating our mind and enlivening our spirits (this effect has been proved scientifically).

Elements of Classical Music:

Melody

The lyrics are tuned in a particular fashion, through which we sing the song. A song is composed by arranging the notes in harmony. The tune formed as a result of combining the pitch and the rhythm is known as the melody. The melody of the song is responsible for making it pleasing to our senses.

Melody is one of the foundational elements of classical music, serving as the central thread that weaves together the various components of a musical composition. At its core, melody can be understood as the sequence of musical notes arranged in a particular order to create a cohesive and expressive musical line. It is the element of a piece of music that is most readily recognizable and memorable to the listener, often serving as the focal point around which other musical elements, such as harmony, rhythm, and texture, revolve.

One of the distinguishing features of melody is its reliance on pitch, which refers to the perceived highness or lowness of a musical sound. The arrangement of pitches in a melody forms a distinctive pattern that gives the music its characteristic shape and identity. Melodies can vary widely in their pitch content, encompassing both simple, stepwise progressions and complex, intervallic leaps. The choice of pitches within a melody can evoke a range of emotions and moods, from joy and exuberance to melancholy and introspection.

In addition to pitch, rhythm plays a crucial role in shaping the contour and flow of a melody. Rhythm refers to the temporal organization of musical sounds, including the duration and placement of notes within a musical phrase. A well-crafted melody strikes a delicate balance between rhythmic variety and coherence, incorporating a combination of long and short durations to create a sense of forward momentum and rhythmic vitality. The rhythmic patterns within a melody contribute to its overall character and energy, shaping the listener's experience of the music.

Furthermore, the structure of a melody often follows established musical forms and conventions, such as the use of repetition, variation, and development to create cohesion and unity within a composition. Repetition involves the recurrence of musical ideas or motifs, providing a sense of familiarity and continuity throughout the piece. Variation introduces subtle changes to the melody, altering its pitch, rhythm, or texture to add interest and complexity. Development involves the gradual unfolding and elaboration of musical themes, exploring new harmonic and melodic territory to create tension and resolution.

The emotional impact of a melody is closely tied to its expressive qualities, including dynamics, articulation, and phrasing. Dynamics refer to the varying degrees of loudness and softness within a melody, which can convey a wide range of emotions, from intensity and passion to subtlety and intimacy. Articulation encompasses the manner in which individual notes are played or sung, including legato (smooth and connected) and staccato (short and detached), which contribute to the overall character and texture of the melody. Phrasing involves the shaping and contouring of musical phrases, creating a sense of tension and release that guides the listener through the narrative arc of the melody.

Melody is a fundamental element of classical music that encompasses pitch, rhythm, structure, and expression. It serves as the primary vehicle for conveying musical ideas, emotions, and themes, capturing the listener's imagination and engaging the senses on a deep and profound level. Through its interplay with other musical elements, melody shapes the overall character and aesthetic of a composition, leaving a lasting impression on the listener long after the music has ended.

Phrase

Basically there are two types of phrases, viz. complete and incomplete. The recurrent musical series are compiled into different phrases that complete the song. The first phrase is followed by the second (cadence), which finally closes the song.

In the realm of music, a phrase serves as a fundamental building block, shaping the structure and narrative flow of a musical composition. Defined by its rhythmic and melodic contours, a phrase can be thought of as a musical sentence, conveying a coherent musical idea or theme within a larger context. Within the framework of classical music, phrases play a vital role in organizing musical material and guiding the listener through the ebb and flow of the music.

One of the distinguishing features of phrases is their ability to convey a sense of musical completeness and closure. In classical music, phrases are typically categorized into two main types: complete and incomplete. A complete phrase is characterized by a clear beginning, middle, and end, forming a self-contained musical unit that provides a sense of resolution or fulfilment. This sense of closure is often achieved through the use of cadences, which are musical punctuation marks that signal the end of a phrase or musical section. Cadences can take various forms, including authentic cadences, plagal cadences, and deceptive cadences, each imparting a distinct sense of finality and resolution.

In contrast, an incomplete phrase lacks a definitive sense of closure or resolution, leaving the listener with a sense of anticipation or expectancy. Incomplete phrases may end abruptly or trail off into silence, creating a sense of tension and ambiguity that invites further development or elaboration. These open-ended phrases play an important role in creating musical tension and drama, allowing composers to manipulate the listener's expectations and shape the overall trajectory of the music.

The relationship between complete and incomplete phrases is central to the formal organization of classical music, providing composers with a flexible framework for structuring their compositions. By juxtaposing contrasting phrases and manipulating their lengths and shapes, composers can create dynamic musical narratives that engage the listener's attention and imagination. This interplay between closure and openness, tension and release, lies at the heart of classical music's expressive power and emotional impact.

Moreover, phrases serve as the building blocks of larger musical forms and structures, such as sonata-allegro form, theme and variations, and rondo form. These formal frameworks provide composers with a blueprint for organizing musical material on a larger scale, allowing them to develop and transform musical ideas over the course of an entire composition. Within these formal structures, phrases serve as the primary means of thematic development and variation, providing composers with a rich palette of musical material to draw upon and manipulate.

Phrases are essential elements of classical music, serving as the basic units of musical expression and organization. Whether complete or incomplete, phrases play a crucial role in shaping the structure, narrative flow, and expressive character of a composition. Through their rhythmic and melodic contours, phrases guide the listener through the musical journey, imparting a sense of coherence, tension, and resolution that lies at the heart of classical music's enduring appeal.

Theme

Classical music is always based on a particular theme, which gets exposed from the lyrics and the melody. A song without a theme is never complete. There might be variation in the themes; nevertheless, it forms the backbone of the song. The theme of the song is generated either spontaneously or by keeping the background into consideration.

In the rich tapestry of classical music, the theme stands as a cornerstone, a foundational element upon which compositions are built and developed. Often emerging from the interplay of melody and lyrics, the theme serves as the central motif around which musical ideas revolve, providing coherence, unity, and direction to the overall structure of a piece. Indeed, a song without a theme is akin to a story without a plot—a formless and disjointed expression lacking in depth and substance.

At its essence, the theme encapsulates the essence of a musical composition, embodying its emotional, narrative, and expressive core. Whether simple or complex, poignant or exuberant, the theme serves as a musical fingerprint, uniquely identifying and defining each composition with its distinctive character and identity. Through its melodic contours, rhythmic patterns, and harmonic progression, the theme evokes a particular mood, atmosphere, or sentiment, inviting listeners on a journey of exploration and discovery.

The genesis of a theme may vary, arising from a myriad of sources and inspirations. In some instances, the theme emerges spontaneously from the creative imagination of the composer, a product of their innermost thoughts, emotions, and experiences. Drawing upon a wellspring of inspiration, composers channel their creative energies into crafting melodies and motifs that resonate with personal meaning and significance, infusing their compositions with a sense of authenticity and depth.

Alternatively, the theme may be derived from external sources or contextual considerations, reflecting broader cultural, historical, or literary influences. Composers often draw upon folk melodies, dance rhythms, or literary themes as a basis for their compositions, incorporating elements of tradition and heritage into their musical tapestry. Through this process of thematic borrowing and adaptation, composers infuse their compositions with layers of meaning and resonance, enriching the musical landscape with a diverse array of themes and motifs.

Once established, the theme serves as the organizing principle around which the composition unfolds, guiding the listener through a series of musical transformations and developments. Composers employ a variety of techniques to explore and elaborate upon the theme, including repetition, variation, and development. Through these creative strategies, composers imbue their compositions with depth, complexity, and nuance, weaving a tapestry of musical ideas that captivates the imagination and engages the senses.

Moreover, the theme serves as a unifying thread that ties together disparate elements within a composition, forging connections between different sections, movements, or characters. Whether manifested as a recurring motif, a leitmotif, or a thematic transformation, the theme serves as a point of reference and continuity, anchoring the listener's experience and providing a sense of coherence and cohesion amidst the diversity of musical expression.

The theme occupies a central position within the landscape of classical music, serving as a beacon of creativity, expression, and meaning. Through its melodic richness, emotional depth, and narrative resonance, the theme captures the essence of a composition, infusing it with vitality, vitality, and purpose. As a timeless and universal symbol of musical artistry, the theme continues to inspire and enchant listeners, inviting them on a journey of discovery and delight through the boundless realm of classical music.

Motif

Motif is the shortest subsection of the melody or the theme. It's a smallest idea or the smallest element of the song comprising three to four notes. Motifs are two types, viz, rhythmic motif and melodic motif. Listen to Beethoven's 5th symphony 'du du du duuuu' to understand what exactly motif is.

In the vast tapestry of musical composition, motifs serve as the building blocks upon which melodies and themes are constructed, providing composers with a palette of musical ideas and gestures to draw upon and develop. Defined by their brevity and distinctiveness, motifs are the smallest discernible units within a musical composition, comprising just a few notes or rhythmic patterns. Despite their compact size, motifs play a crucial role in shaping the overall structure, character, and expressive content of a piece, imbuing it with richness, coherence, and unity.

At its essence, a motif can be understood as a musical idea or gesture that recurs throughout a composition, serving as a point of reference and continuity amidst the diversity of musical material. Often derived from the thematic material or melodic contours of a composition, motifs encapsulate the essence of a musical idea in its simplest and most elemental form. Whether melodic or rhythmic in nature, motifs embody a particular mood, atmosphere, or sentiment, evoking a sense of familiarity and resonance within the listener.

One of the defining characteristics of motifs is their brevity and succinctness, typically comprising just a few notes or rhythmic patterns.

This economy of expression allows motifs to convey musical ideas with clarity and precision, making them easily recognizable and memorable to the listener. Moreover, the compact size of motifs enables composers to manipulate and transform them in various ways, incorporating them into different contexts and settings to create new musical meanings and associations.

Motifs can take various forms, including melodic motifs and rhythmic motifs, each serving a distinct role in the compositional process. Melodic motifs consist of a sequence of pitches or tones that form a distinctive melodic pattern or gesture. These melodic fragments may be repeated, varied, or developed over the course of a composition, creating thematic unity and coherence. Rhythmic motifs, on the other hand, are characterized by a recurring rhythmic pattern or pulse that provides a sense of rhythmic drive and momentum to the music. These rhythmic patterns may be syncopated, irregular, or asymmetrical, adding interest and complexity to the rhythmic texture of a composition.

One of the most famous examples of a motif in classical music can be found in Ludwig van Beethoven's Symphony No. 5 in C minor, Op. 67, commonly known as the "Fate Symphony." The opening motif of this symphony, consisting of three short notes followed by a long note (often described as "du du du duuuu"), has become one of the most iconic and recognizable motifs in the classical repertoire. This simple yet powerful motif recurs throughout the symphony, undergoing various transformations and developments, serving as a unifying thread that ties together the different movements and sections of the composition.

Motifs are essential elements of musical composition, providing composers with a flexible and versatile tool for organizing and developing musical ideas. Whether melodic or rhythmic in nature, motifs serve as the building blocks upon which melodies, themes, and entire compositions are constructed, imbuing them with coherence, unity, and expressive depth. Through their brevity, distinctiveness, and adaptability, motifs enrich the musical experience, inviting listeners on a journey of exploration and discovery through the boundless realm of classical music.

Sonata

Sonata is composed of three main sections 'an exposition, a development, and a recapitulation'. The 'sonata-allegro' became famous during the classical period, which leads to development of many forms of themes of classical music. Many modern classical singers consider sonata to be the good 'model for musical analyses'.

The sonata is a foundational form in classical music, renowned for its structural clarity, thematic development, and expressive depth. Originating in the late Baroque period and reaching its peak during the Classical era, the sonata evolved into a versatile and flexible musical genre, encompassing a wide range of styles, forms, and expressions. Central to the sonata form is its tripartite structure, consisting of three main sections: the exposition, the development, and the recapitulation. This framework provides composers with a framework for organizing and developing musical ideas, creating a narrative arc that guides the listener through a journey of exploration and discovery.

The exposition serves as the opening statement of the sonata form, introducing the primary thematic material and establishing the tonal framework of the composition. Typically divided into two thematic groups or subjects, the exposition presents contrasting musical ideas in different keys, providing a sense of tension and contrast that sets the stage for the subsequent development and elaboration. The first subject is often characterized by its boldness, clarity, and assertiveness, while the second subject offers a contrasting perspective, introducing new melodic material, harmonic colours, and emotional nuances. Together, these thematic groups lay the foundation for the unfolding narrative of the sonata, inviting listeners on a journey of thematic exploration and transformation.

Following the exposition, the development section represents the heart of the sonata form, offering composers the opportunity to explore and expand upon the thematic material introduced in the opening statement. In this section, composers engage in a process of musical development, manipulating, fragmenting, and transforming the thematic material in a variety of ways to create tension, contrast, and drama. Through techniques such as fragmentation, sequence, modulation, and thematic transformation, composers push the boundaries of tonality and form, blurring the lines between different keys and musical ideas. The development section is characterized by its sense of freedom, experimentation, and unpredictability, allowing composers to unleash their creative energies and explore new musical territories.

Finally, the recapitulation brings the sonata form full circle, restating and reimagining the thematic material introduced in the exposition within the context of a unified tonal framework. Unlike the exposition, where the thematic material is presented in contrasting keys, the recapitulation restates the thematic material in the tonic key, providing a sense of closure and resolution that brings the composition to a satisfying conclusion. While the thematic material remains largely unchanged, composers may introduce subtle variations, elaborations, or reinterpretations to imbue the recapitulation with freshness and vitality. Through this process of recapitulation, composers reaffirm the central themes and ideas of the sonata, reinforcing the structural integrity and coherence of the composition.

Throughout its history, the sonata form has served as a model for musical analysis and compositional technique, inspiring generations of composers to explore new possibilities and push the boundaries of artistic expression. From the classical masters such as Mozart, Beethoven, and Haydn to the modern innovators of the 20th and 21st centuries, composers have drawn upon the rich legacy of the sonata form to create works of timeless beauty, complexity, and significance. Today, the sonata form continues to captivate and inspire audiences around the world, reminding us of the enduring power and relevance of classical music in the contemporary age.

Measure

The time span (time signature) of the music within which the lyrics are composed harmoniously is known as the measure. It's also known as the bar of the music notation. In short, it is the 'beat per duration'. The entire duration of the music further depends on its lyrics and tune.

In the intricate world of music notation, the measure stands as a fundamental unit of organization, providing composers, performers, and listeners with a framework for understanding and interpreting the rhythmic structure of a musical composition. Also known as the bar, the measure serves as a rhythmic container within which musical events unfold, delineating the passage of time and establishing a sense of pulse and meter. From the lively dance rhythms of a Mozart minuet to the sweeping melodies of a Beethoven symphony, the measure plays a crucial role in shaping the rhythmic landscape of classical music, imbuing it with vitality, coherence, and expressive depth.

At its core, the measure is defined by its time span, which is determined by the time signature or meter of the music. The time signature consists of two numbers written at the beginning of a musical score, indicating the number of beats per measure and the type of note that receives one beat. For example, a time signature of 4/4 indicates that there are four beats per measure, with the quarter note receiving one beat. Similarly, a time signature of 3/4 signifies three beats per measure, with the quarter note still receiving one beat. These time signatures provide a rhythmic framework within which composers can organize their musical material, allowing them to create rhythmic patterns, accents, and phrasing that give shape and structure to the music.

Within each measure, the beats are further subdivided into smaller rhythmic units, such as eighth notes, sixteenth notes, and triplets, each contributing to the overall rhythmic complexity and texture of the music. These rhythmic subdivisions provide composers with a palette of expressive possibilities, allowing them to create intricate rhythmic patterns, syncopations, and polyrhythms that add interest and depth to the music. By varying the rhythmic density and distribution of notes within each measure, composers can shape the rhythmic character of their compositions, evoking different moods, emotions, and musical effects.

Moreover, the measure serves as a structural marker within the musical score, helping performers navigate the rhythmic landscape of the music and interpret it with precision and clarity. Musicians rely on the measure as a reference point for counting beats, coordinating entrances and exits, and maintaining rhythmic cohesion within an ensemble. Whether performing as a soloist, chamber musician, or orchestral player, musicians use the measure as a guidepost for navigating the rhythmic complexities of the music, ensuring that each note is played with precision and accuracy.

In addition to its practical function, the measure also has symbolic significance within the realm of musical aesthetics and interpretation. The measure serves as a metaphor for the passage of time and the cyclical nature of musical experience, reflecting the rhythm of life itself. Through its rhythmic regularity and predictability, the measure provides a sense of order and stability amidst the chaos and uncertainty of the world, offering listeners a sense of comfort and reassurance. As listeners immerse themselves in the rhythmic pulse of the music, they become attuned to its underlying patterns and cycles, experiencing a profound sense of connection and resonance with the music and its expressive content.

The measure stands as a foundational element of music notation, providing composers, performers, and listeners with a rhythmic framework for organizing and interpreting musical material. From its role in establishing pulse and meter to its function as a structural marker within the musical score, the measure plays a crucial role in shaping the rhythmic landscape of classical music, imbuing it with vitality, coherence, and expressive depth. Through its rhythmic regularity and symbolic resonance, the measure invites listeners on a journey of rhythmic exploration and discovery, enriching their musical experience and deepening their appreciation for the timeless beauty of classical music.

Timbre

It's the quality of individual notes that helps in distinguishing one from another. The sound produced from the musical instrument depends upon the quality of the timbre used. Timbre is also connoted as *tone color* and *tone quality*, and due to this the notes produced have a differential effect.

In the rich tapestry of music, timbre stands as a cornerstone of sonic identity, shaping the unique quality and character of individual notes and instruments. Often referred to as tone colour or tone quality, timbre encompasses a broad spectrum of auditory characteristics that distinguish one sound from another, lending each note its own distinctive hue, texture, and expressive resonance. From the warm, velvety tones of a cello to the bright, shimmering timbres of a flute, timbre plays a crucial role in shaping the sonic landscape of music, imbuing it with richness, depth, and complexity.

At its essence, timbre can be understood as the unique fingerprint of a sound, resulting from the complex interplay of various acoustic properties, including frequency spectrum, amplitude envelope, and harmonic content. Unlike pitch, which refers to the perceived highness or lowness of a sound, timbre encompasses a wide range of perceptual dimensions, including brightness, richness, roughness, and clarity. These dimensions are influenced by a variety of factors, including the size, shape, and material properties of the sound-producing source, as well as the techniques and articulations employed by the performer.

One of the defining characteristics of timbre is its subjective and multidimensional nature, which makes it difficult to quantify or describe in precise terms. While pitch can be represented by a single frequency value, timbre defies such simplistic categorization, encompassing a multitude of sonic nuances and subtleties that elude easy classification. Indeed, the richness and complexity of timbre lie in its capacity to evoke a wide range of emotions, associations, and sensations, from the warmth and intimacy of a human voice to the ethereal beauty of a string quartet.

Moreover, timbre serves as a powerful expressive tool for composers and performers, allowing them to convey mood, emotion, and narrative through the subtle manipulation of sonic colour and texture. Composers often exploit the expressive potential of timbre to create evocative sonic landscapes, using timbral contrasts, juxtapositions, and transformations to shape the dramatic arc of a musical composition. Performers, in turn, draw upon a rich palette of timbral techniques and articulations to infuse their interpretations with depth, nuance, and personality, breathing life into the notes and bringing the music to vivid, vibrant life.

In addition to its expressive qualities, timbre also plays a crucial role in facilitating auditory perception and cognition, providing listeners with valuable cues and clues for making sense of the sonic environment. By attending to the timbral characteristics of sounds, listeners are able to distinguish between different instruments, voices, and musical styles, enabling them to navigate and interpret complex musical textures with ease and confidence. Moreover, timbre contributes to the aesthetic experience of music, enhancing its sensory appeal and enriching its emotional impact.

Timbre stands as a multifaceted and dynamic aspect of music, shaping the unique identity and expressive richness of individual notes and instruments. From its role in conveying mood and emotion to its function in facilitating auditory perception and cognition, timbre plays a crucial role in shaping the sonic landscape of music, imbuing it with vitality, depth, and complexity. As listeners immerse themselves in the rich tapestry of timbral colours and textures, they embark on a journey of sonic exploration and discovery, experiencing the transformative power and beauty of music in all its myriad forms.

Meter

The total number of syllables, lines, accents and rhythm in the music forms the meter. The technical terms used for defining a meter are *measured rhythm*, *rhythmic shape* and *time*. Meter results from arrangement of these elements. The melody of the song gets affected if the meter is not well measured.

Meter, often considered the heartbeat of music, plays a crucial role in defining the structure and flow of a composition. It is the framework that organizes the rhythm, accents, and beats within a piece, giving it shape and direction. Meter in music is composed of several key elements: syllables, lines, accents, and rhythm. Each of these components contributes to the overall structure and feel of a piece. In vocal music, syllables refer to the individual units of sound within the lyrics. The arrangement and emphasis of syllables within a line can influence the natural rhythm of the music. Lines in music often correspond to phrases or measures in a composition. The length and grouping of these lines contribute to the overall meter, determining how the music flows from one section to the next. Accents are the emphases placed on certain beats or notes. They help to create a pattern within the rhythm, guiding the listener's perception of the meter. Rhythm is the pattern of sounds and silences in music. It is the temporal aspect that dictates the timing of notes and rests, forming the basis of the meter.

The technical terms used to define meter are "measured rhythm," "rhythmic shape," and "time." Measured rhythm refers to the precise timing and duration of notes and rests within a piece. It is the structured aspect of rhythm that can be notated and measured, often represented by time signatures in written music. Rhythmic shape describes the overall contour and pattern of the rhythm. It encompasses the combination of long and short notes, as well as the placement of accents, creating a distinctive rhythmic identity for a piece. In musical terminology, "time" is often synonymous with the time signature, which indicates how many beats are in each measure and what note value constitutes one beat. Common time signatures include 4/4, 3/4, and 6/8, each providing a different framework for the meter.

Meter is not merely a theoretical construct; it has practical implications for the performance and perception of music. It provides a framework that organizes the various elements of music, dividing a composition into manageable segments, making it easier for musicians to read, interpret, and perform. A well-defined meter creates a sense of predictability, allowing listeners to anticipate the flow of the music, which is essential for creating rhythmic coherence and maintaining the listener's engagement. The choice of meter can significantly affect the emotional tone of a piece. For example, a waltz in 3/4 time often conveys a light, flowing feeling, while a march in 4/4 time tends to feel more structured and determined. Varying the meter or incorporating irregular meters can add complexity and interest to a piece. Composers often use changes in meter to highlight different sections of a composition or to create a sense of tension and release.

The meter must be carefully measured and maintained throughout a piece. Any inconsistencies or inaccuracies can disrupt the flow and coherence of the music, leading to several potential issues. If the meter is not well measured, the melody may feel disjointed or awkward, compromising the natural phrasing and flow of the music, affecting the overall aesthetic. Musicians rely on a consistent meter to maintain their timing and coordination, and an improperly measured meter can create difficulties in performance, leading to mistakes and a lack of synchronization. For the audience, an inconsistent meter can be confusing and jarring, making the music harder to follow and diminishing the listener's enjoyment and appreciation.

Meter is a foundational element in music, essential for creating structure, coherence, and emotional impact. By understanding the components and technical aspects of meter, musicians and composers can craft pieces that are rhythmically engaging and aesthetically pleasing. Proper measurement and maintenance of meter ensure that the melody and overall composition flow seamlessly, allowing both performers and listeners to fully experience the intended expression of the music. As such, meter is not just a theoretical concept but a practical tool that shapes the very essence of musical artistry.

Harmony

What makes a classical song so harmonious? It's the harmony. The chords, pitches, tones and notes when blended perfectly create the best type of music. Harmony adds texture and quality to classical music. It's done by tuning the chord and adding the desired tension to it, so that the sound produced is soothing and melodious.

Harmony is the cornerstone of classical music, imparting a sense of balance and beauty that distinguishes it from other genres. The essence of harmony lies in the intricate interplay of chords, pitches, tones, and notes, which, when blended perfectly, create a resonant and enriching musical experience. Chords, the building blocks of harmony, consist of multiple notes played simultaneously, creating a depth of sound that can evoke a wide range of emotions. By carefully selecting and arranging these chords, composers can craft music that is both soothing and complex. The pitches, or specific frequencies of these notes, are meticulously chosen to complement each other, ensuring that they sound pleasing when played together.

The tones, which refer to the quality or colour of the sound produced, also play a crucial role in harmony. Different instruments produce different tones, and the combination of these tones adds texture and richness to the music. In classical music, composers often use a variety of instruments to create a harmonious blend of tones, from the bright sound of the violin to the warm, mellow tones of the cello. This interplay of tones creates a layered and dynamic soundscape that enhances the overall listening experience.

Notes, the fundamental units of music, are combined in specific sequences and patterns to form melodies and harmonies. The arrangement of these notes within a chord and their progression throughout a piece is what gives classical music its distinctive harmonic structure. Composers use various techniques, such as counterpoint and modulation, to create tension and release within the music, adding to its emotional depth and complexity. Counterpoint involves the interaction of independent musical lines, each with its own melody, that come together to create a cohesive harmonic texture. Modulation, or the change from one key to another, introduces new harmonic possibilities and keeps the music engaging and dynamic.

Harmony adds texture and quality to classical music by providing a framework within which melodies can develop and interact. It creates a sense of movement and direction, guiding the listener through the different sections of a piece. This is achieved by tuning the chords and adding the desired tension to them, ensuring that the sound produced is both soothing and melodious. Tension in music is created by the use of dissonance, or notes that clash when played together, which resolves into consonance, or harmonious sound, creating a sense of resolution and satisfaction. This interplay of tension and resolution is a key aspect of classical music's harmonic structure, giving it its unique emotional impact.

The process of tuning chords involves adjusting the pitch of each note to ensure that they are in perfect harmony with each other. This requires a deep understanding of musical theory and an acute sense of hearing. Composers and musicians must listen carefully to the intervals, or the distance between notes, and make subtle adjustments to achieve the desired harmonic effect. This attention to detail is what allows classical music to achieve such a high level of harmonic sophistication and beauty.

Harmony in classical music is not just about creating a pleasing sound; it also serves to enhance the expressive power of the music. By carefully manipulating the harmonic structure, composers can convey a wide range of emotions, from joy and excitement to sadness and longing. The use of minor chords, for example, often evokes a sense of melancholy or introspection, while major chords can create a feeling of happiness and triumph. The combination of different harmonic elements allows composers to create music that is rich in emotional content and capable of deeply moving the listener.

The historical development of harmony in classical music has been marked by continuous innovation and refinement. From the simple, monophonic chants of the medieval period to the complex polyphony of the Renaissance, and from the harmonic experimentation of the Baroque era to the lush, expressive harmonies of the Romantic period, composers have constantly pushed the boundaries of what is possible with harmony. Each period brought new techniques and approaches to harmony, expanding the expressive potential of classical music and contributing to its rich and diverse legacy.

In the Baroque period, for example, composers like Johann Sebastian Bach developed complex harmonic structures using techniques such as figured bass and the use of basso continuo, where a continuous bass line provides a harmonic foundation for the music. This period also saw the development of functional harmony, where chords are used in a hierarchical system to create a sense of progression and resolution. The Classical period, exemplified by composers such as Wolfgang Amadeus Mozart and Ludwig van Beethoven, refined these techniques, creating music that is characterized by clarity, balance, and formal elegance.

The Romantic period, with composers like Johannes Brahms and Richard Wagner, pushed the boundaries of harmony even further, using chromaticism and extended chords to create music that is rich in emotional depth and complexity.

Harmony in classical music also involves the use of specific forms and structures that organize the harmonic content of a piece. Sonata form, for example, is a common structure used in classical music that consists of an exposition, development, and recapitulation. This form allows for the presentation and exploration of different harmonic ideas, creating a sense of coherence and unity within the music. Other forms, such as the fugue and the rondo, also use specific harmonic structures to create a sense of order and progression.

The role of the performer in achieving harmony in classical music cannot be overstated. Performers must have a deep understanding of the harmonic structure of the music they are playing, as well as the technical skill to execute it accurately. This involves not only playing the correct notes but also paying attention to dynamics, articulation, and phrasing to bring out the harmonic nuances of the music. The interaction between different performers in an ensemble is also crucial, as they must listen to each other and adjust their playing to create a cohesive and harmonious sound.

It is the foundation of classical music, providing the structure and depth that make it so captivating and emotionally powerful. The careful blending of chords, pitches, tones, and notes creates a rich and textured sound that can evoke a wide range of emotions. Through techniques such as counterpoint and modulation, and the use of forms and structures, composers are able to create music that is both complex and cohesive. The historical development of harmony has seen continuous innovation, with each period bringing new techniques and approaches that have expanded the expressive potential of classical music. Performers play a crucial role in realizing the harmonic potential of a piece, requiring both technical skill and a deep understanding of the music. Harmony in classical music is not just about creating a pleasing sound, but about conveying emotion and telling a story, making it an essential element of this timeless and beloved genre.

Coda

You can define coda as an extension of a cadence that paves the way for completing the music. It's the concluding part of the music and is usually placed towards the end of the composition e.g. C Major Sonata in Mozart's classical pieces.

The coda, derived from the Italian word for "tail," is an essential element in musical composition, particularly within classical music. It functions as an extension of a cadence, providing a pathway to bring a piece to a satisfying and coherent conclusion. The coda is typically situated at the end of a composition, serving as the final statement that encapsulates the thematic and harmonic material presented throughout the piece. It is not merely an afterthought or a simple closing remark but a thoughtfully crafted section that ties together the musical narrative, often adding depth and resolution.

In the context of classical music, the coda holds a significant place in the structural and expressive design of a composition. Composers use the coda to reinforce the primary themes and motifs introduced earlier, often revisiting and elaborating on them to create a sense of closure. This revisiting helps to solidify the listener's experience, ensuring that the musical ideas are thoroughly explored and resolved. For instance, in the C Major Sonata by Wolfgang Amadeus Mozart, the coda is not just a perfunctory ending but a vital part of the composition's architecture. Mozart utilizes the coda to reiterate the sonata's main themes while also introducing subtle variations and developments, thereby enhancing the listener's understanding and appreciation of the piece.

The role of the coda extends beyond mere repetition; it often involves significant harmonic and rhythmic development. Composers may introduce new material or transform existing themes in unexpected ways, creating a dynamic and engaging conclusion. This process of transformation and development can heighten the emotional impact of the music, providing a sense of culmination and finality. In some compositions, the coda can be expansive and elaborate, almost serving as a miniature movement in its own right, while in others, it might be brief and succinct, providing a concise and poignant ending.

The harmonic structure of a coda is crucial in achieving its purpose. By resolving harmonic tensions and leading the music back to the tonic, the coda creates a sense of completeness and satisfaction. This harmonic resolution is often achieved through cadential progressions that reaffirm the home key, providing a clear and definitive endpoint. The use of strong cadences, such as the perfect or plagal cadence, helps to anchor the music and deliver a powerful sense of closure. Additionally, the coda may employ varied harmonic techniques, including modulations and chromaticism, to enrich the musical texture and maintain the listener's interest until the very end.

Rhythmically, the coda can play with expectations and provide a final burst of energy or a gentle winding down, depending on the desired emotional effect. Composers might use rhythmic motifs from earlier in the piece, weaving them into the coda to create a cohesive and unified conclusion. The interplay of rhythmic patterns can generate excitement and anticipation, leading to a dramatic and memorable finale. Alternatively, a more subdued rhythmic approach can evoke a sense of calm and resolution, allowing the music to fade gracefully into silence.

The coda's significance is further highlighted in its ability to balance and complement the preceding sections of a composition. It acts as a counterweight to the introduction, development, and recapitulation, ensuring that the musical journey feels complete and well-rounded. By revisiting key themes and motifs, the coda provides a sense of symmetry and closure, reinforcing the structural integrity of the piece. This balance is essential in classical compositions, where formal structure and thematic coherence are paramount.

In addition to its structural role, the coda also serves an expressive function. It allows composers to convey a final emotional statement, encapsulating the mood and character of the entire composition. Whether conveying triumph, serenity, or introspection, the coda provides a platform for the composer to leave a lasting impression on the listener. This expressive quality is often achieved through the use of dynamic contrasts, melodic embellishments, and textural variations, which add richness and depth to the concluding section.

The historical development of the coda in classical music reflects its evolving significance. During the Baroque period, codas were often brief and functional, serving primarily to conclude a piece in a tidy manner. However, as musical forms became more sophisticated in the Classical and Romantic periods, the coda evolved into a more elaborate and integral component of the composition. Composers like Ludwig van Beethoven and Franz Schubert expanded the scope and complexity of codas, using them to explore new thematic material and provide a more profound resolution. Beethoven, in particular, is renowned for his extensive and innovative codas, which often transform and elevate the music in surprising ways.

In Beethoven's symphonies and sonatas, the coda frequently serves as a culmination of the entire movement, bringing together various themes and motifs in a grand and conclusive manner. For example, the coda in the final movement of Beethoven's Symphony No. 5 in C minor is a powerful and triumphant conclusion, reinforcing the symphony's overarching theme of struggle and victory. By extending the coda and incorporating dramatic developments, Beethoven creates a sense of epic resolution that leaves a lasting impact on the listener.

The Romantic period saw further developments in the use of codas, with composers like Johannes Brahms and Richard Wagner incorporating them into their symphonic and operatic works. Brahms often used the coda to revisit and reinterpret earlier themes, providing a reflective and introspective conclusion. Wagner, on the other hand, utilized the coda to achieve dramatic and theatrical effects, heightening the emotional intensity of his operatic finales.

In contemporary classical music, the coda continues to be an important structural and expressive element. Modern composers often experiment with the traditional concept of the coda, incorporating innovative harmonic, rhythmic, and textural techniques. While the fundamental purpose of the coda as a concluding section remains, its execution can vary widely, reflecting the diverse approaches and styles of contemporary music.

The coda is a vital component of classical music, serving as the final extension of a cadence that paves the way for completing a composition. It provides a sense of closure and resolution, reinforcing the thematic and harmonic material presented throughout the piece. Through careful selection and arrangement of chords, pitches, tones, and notes, the coda creates a harmonious and satisfying conclusion. Its structural and expressive functions ensure that the musical narrative is complete, leaving a lasting impression on the listener. From the brief and functional codas of the Baroque period to the elaborate and innovative codas of Beethoven and beyond, the coda has evolved into a crucial element of musical composition, reflecting the depth and richness of classical music.

Rhythm

The uniform motion that music follows to progress is known as the rhythm of the music. The notes recur, new notes are generated and the music keeps flowing in a particular fashion, which is known as the rhythm. The rhythm of the music is also created by the beats.

Rhythm is the driving force behind music, providing the structure and motion that propel it forward. It is the organized pattern of sounds and silences that dictates the flow and progression of a piece, much like a heartbeat maintains the pulse of a living being. Rhythm is fundamental to all forms of music, serving as the backbone that supports melody and harmony. It is characterized by the recurrence of notes and the generation of new ones, creating a dynamic and evolving sequence that guides the listener through the composition. This orderly sequence, or rhythmic pattern, ensures that the music flows in a coherent and predictable manner, making it comprehensible and engaging.

At its core, rhythm is generated by beats, which are the basic units of time in music. Beats provide a steady pulse that can be felt throughout a piece, often grouped into measures or bars by time signatures. The time signature indicates how many beats are in each measure and what type of note represents one beat. Common time signatures, such as 4/4, 3/4, and 6/8, each impart a distinct rhythmic character to the music. For instance, a 4/4 time signature, often called common time, is pervasive in Western music and provides a straightforward, steady rhythm. In contrast, a 3/4 time signature, characteristic of waltzes, creates a lilting, dance-like feel.

Rhythm is not only about the placement of beats but also about the duration and emphasis of notes within these beats. Notes of varying lengths—whole notes, half notes, quarter notes, eighth notes, and so on—combine to form different rhythmic patterns. The duration of notes and rests (silences) interspersed between them contributes to the overall texture and complexity of the rhythm. Syncopation, where the emphasis is placed on typically weak beats or off-beats, adds an element of surprise and interest to the music, disrupting the regular flow and creating a more engaging rhythmic experience.

Accents, or the emphasis on certain beats, further shape the rhythm. By stressing particular notes or beats, composers can create a sense of movement and energy within the music. These accents often align with the natural phrasing of the melody, reinforcing its structure and making it more expressive. The interplay between accented and unaccented beats helps to define the rhythmic character of a piece, contributing to its overall mood and style.

Beyond the basic beat and note duration, rhythm encompasses more complex elements like tempo and meter. Tempo, the speed at which a piece of music is played, has a profound impact on its rhythmic feel. A fast tempo can generate excitement and urgency, while a slow tempo may evoke calmness or solemnity. Composers often use tempo changes to alter the emotional landscape of a piece, guiding the listener through different moods and sections. Meter, the grouping of beats into regular patterns, also influences the rhythm. Simple meters, like duple (2/4) or triple (3/4) meter, provide straightforward rhythmic foundations, while compound meters, like 6/8 or 9/8, introduce more intricate patterns that can create a sense of fluidity or complexity.

Rhythm is also closely tied to the concept of groove, particularly in genres like jazz, funk, and rock. Groove refers to the feel of the rhythm, the way it compels the listener to move or dance. It is created through the interaction of various rhythmic elements, including the placement of beats, syncopation, and the interplay between different instruments. A strong groove can make a piece of music irresistibly compelling, engaging listeners on a visceral level.

In classical music, rhythm plays a crucial role in defining the form and structure of compositions. Different sections of a piece, such as the exposition, development, and recapitulation in sonata form, often feature distinct rhythmic patterns that contribute to their unique identities. Rhythmic motifs, short rhythmic phrases that recur throughout a piece, can serve as unifying elements, linking different sections and creating a sense of coherence. Composers like Ludwig van Beethoven and Igor Stravinsky are renowned for their innovative use of rhythm, employing complex and varied rhythmic structures to add depth and excitement to their music.

Rhythmic variation is another important aspect of rhythm in music. By altering the rhythmic patterns, composers can create contrast and maintain the listener's interest. This can involve changing the note values, introducing syncopation, or shifting the meter. Such variations prevent the music from becoming monotonous and help to highlight different sections and themes. In many cases, rhythmic variation is used to develop motifs and ideas introduced earlier in the piece, adding layers of complexity and richness to the music.

In addition to its structural and expressive roles, rhythm also has a profound psychological and physiological impact on listeners. The regularity and predictability of rhythm can induce a state of relaxation or focus, while more complex and unexpected rhythms can stimulate excitement and alertness. This is why rhythm is such a powerful tool in various contexts, from the meditative rhythms of ambient music to the driving beats of dance music.

In the realm of performance, rhythm requires precise timing and coordination. Musicians must internalize the rhythmic structure of a piece, maintaining a steady pulse while navigating complex patterns and syncopations. Ensemble playing, in particular, demands a high level of rhythmic synchronization, as players must align their rhythms to create a cohesive and unified sound. Conductors often play a key role in guiding the rhythm of an orchestra, using their gestures to indicate tempo, meter, and accents.

Rhythm also plays a crucial role in non-Western musical traditions, where it can be even more complex and integral to the music. For example, in Indian classical music, rhythm (or "tala") is a central component, with intricate patterns and cycles that are foundational to the performance. African music is renowned for its polyrhythms, where multiple contrasting rhythmic patterns are played simultaneously, creating a rich and interlocking tapestry of sound. These diverse rhythmic practices highlight the universal importance of rhythm in music and its ability to convey a wide range of cultural expressions and emotions.

In conclusion, rhythm is the uniform motion that music follows to progress, the organized pattern of sounds and silences that gives music its structure and flow. It is generated by beats and shaped by the duration, emphasis, and arrangement of notes. Rhythm encompasses elements like tempo and meter, which influence the speed and grouping of beats, and it plays a crucial role in defining the form and emotional impact of music. Through rhythmic variation and the interplay of accents and syncopation, rhythm adds complexity and interest to a piece, engaging the listener and enhancing the overall musical experience. Its psychological and physiological effects make it a powerful tool for composers and performers alike, ensuring that music remains a dynamic and compelling art form. Whether in the steady pulse of a classical symphony, the intricate patterns of Indian classical music, or the driving beats of contemporary dance music, rhythm is the fundamental force that propels music forward and connects it to the human experience.

These play a significant role in forming the structure and the tune of the song. If you are really fond of classical music, then I'm sure you will try to figure out these elements while listening to a classical song. Play the music and get completely absorbed in its melody.

HOW TO LISTEN TO CLASSICAL MUSIC

Classical music has been an integral part of our lives, directly or indirectly. We have been exposed to many classical music pieces used in commercials, as background music in movies, in cartoons and even in video games. Take an example, a classical piece called *'O Fortuna'*, has been used in various media forms. Also, music pieces by Beethoven and Mozart have been used in cartoons, for example, *'Tom and Jerry'* and in sitcoms, for example, *'South Park'* and *'The Simpsons'*. Ever since we entered school, Beethoven's and Mozart's music was recommended for listening to improve our memory and concentration power, and sometimes serving as a lullaby. I am sure that we all have heard some piece or notes of classical music, even if we didn't know we were listening to it or even if we didn't know who the artist was.

Listening to classical music can be a deeply enriching and transformative experience, but it often requires a different approach compared to other genres. To fully appreciate and enjoy classical music, one must cultivate active listening skills, understand the historical and theoretical context, and be open to the emotional and intellectual journey that the music offers. Here's a comprehensive guide on how to listen to classical music effectively.

First and foremost, it's essential to approach classical music with an open mind and a willingness to engage deeply with the music. Unlike popular music, which often relies on repetitive structures and immediate gratification, classical music can be complex and layered, requiring attentive listening and patience. Start by selecting a quiet and comfortable environment where you can listen without distractions. This will allow you to focus entirely on the music and immerse yourself in the experience.

Begin by familiarizing yourself with the basics of musical structure and terminology. Understanding concepts such as melody, harmony, rhythm, and form can significantly enhance your listening experience. Melody refers to the sequence of notes that are perceived as a single entity, often the most recognizable part of a piece. Harmony is the combination of different musical notes played or sung simultaneously, creating a richer sound. Rhythm is the pattern of sounds and silences in time, providing the temporal framework for the music. Form refers to the overall structure of a piece, including its different sections and how they are organized. Recognizing these elements can help you appreciate the intricacies of a composition.

It's also beneficial to learn about the different periods of classical music, as each era has its own distinct characteristics and styles. The Baroque period (1600-1750), exemplified by composers like Johann Sebastian Bach and George Frideric Handel, is known for its ornate and intricate music. The Classical period (1750-1820), with composers such as Wolfgang Amadeus Mozart and Ludwig van Beethoven, emphasizes clarity, balance, and form. The Romantic period (1820-1900), featuring composers like Johannes Brahms and Richard Wagner, focuses on expressive and emotive music. The 20th century and beyond saw a wide range of styles and innovations, with composers such as Igor Stravinsky and John Cage pushing the boundaries of classical music. Understanding these historical contexts can provide insight into the music's evolution and its cultural significance.

When listening to a piece of classical music, it's helpful to follow the score if you have access to it. This allows you to see the written notation and understand how the music is constructed. If you're not familiar with reading music, you can still benefit from watching visual representations of the music, such as animated scores available online. These visual aids can help you track the different voices and instruments, making it easier to follow complex compositions.

Active listening is crucial in classical music. Pay attention to the different instruments and how they interact with each other. Notice the dynamics, or the variations in loudness and softness, and how they contribute to the emotional impact of the piece. Listen for the motifs and themes, which are recurring musical ideas that provide coherence and unity to the composition. Many classical works, especially symphonies and sonatas, are built around the development of these themes, and recognizing them can enhance your appreciation of the music's structure and ingenuity.

It's also important to understand the emotional and narrative aspects of classical music. Many compositions tell a story or convey a particular mood or atmosphere. For instance, Beethoven's Symphony No. 6, also known as the "Pastoral Symphony," evokes scenes of nature and countryside life. Gustav Mahler's symphonies often explore profound philosophical and existential themes. By connecting with the emotional content of the music, you can experience a deeper and more personal engagement with the piece.

Repetition is a valuable tool in listening to classical music. Don't hesitate to listen to a piece multiple times. Each listening can reveal new details and nuances that you might have missed initially. Over time, you'll develop a deeper understanding and appreciation of the music. Try listening to different interpretations of the same piece by various performers or orchestras. Each interpretation can offer a unique perspective, highlighting different aspects of the music and demonstrating the performers' artistic choices.

Engage with supplementary materials such as program notes, biographies of composers, and historical contexts of the compositions. Many recordings and performances provide detailed program notes that offer insights into the music's background, structure, and significance. Reading about the composer's life and the circumstances under which the piece was written can add layers of meaning to your listening experience.

Attending live performances can significantly enhance your appreciation of classical music. The experience of seeing and hearing an orchestra or soloist perform in person is unparalleled. Pay attention to the conductor's gestures, the musicians' interactions, and the acoustics of the concert hall. Live performances bring a tangible, visceral dimension to the music that recordings cannot fully capture.

Join a community of classical music enthusiasts, such as local music societies, online forums, or social media groups. Discussing your experiences and exchanging insights with others can deepen your understanding and enjoyment of classical music. Many communities offer listening guides, recommended recordings, and educational resources that can further enrich your experience.

Don't be discouraged if you find some pieces challenging or difficult to appreciate at first. Classical music covers a vast and diverse repertoire, and it's natural to have preferences and aversions. Explore different composers, periods, and styles to find what resonates with you. Over time, your tastes may evolve, and you might develop an appreciation for pieces that initially seemed inaccessible.

Finally, approach classical music with curiosity and a sense of exploration. Each piece is a unique work of art, offering a window into the composer's mind and the era in which it was created. By listening attentively and thoughtfully, you can embark on a rewarding journey of musical discovery and personal enrichment.

In conclusion, listening to classical music requires an active, engaged approach that combines an understanding of musical structure, historical context, and emotional content. By creating an ideal listening environment, familiarizing yourself with musical terminology, and exploring different periods and styles, you can deepen your appreciation of classical music. Following the score, paying attention to dynamics and themes, and understanding the narrative aspects of compositions further enhance the experience. Repetition, attending live performances, engaging with supplementary materials, and joining a community of enthusiasts can all contribute to a richer and more fulfilling relationship with classical music. With patience, curiosity, and an open mind, you can unlock the profound beauty and complexity that classical music offers, transforming your listening experience into a journey of discovery and personal growth.

If your dilemma is, that you like listening to heavy metal, psychedelic rock, or pop music and you don't really like listening to classical music, how will you ever develop a liking for it? Then, I am here to tell you *how*. You tried listening to classical music, but couldn't hold on to it for long because it didn't seem fun or intriguing enough, right? This feeling is normal. I went through the same before, and have now discovered my love and interest for it. I am going to explain, how you could listen to classical music and enjoy it, just the way I did.

How to Enjoy Listening to Classical Music

Enjoying classical music can be an immensely rewarding experience that enriches your emotional and intellectual life. To fully appreciate and take pleasure in listening to classical music, it's important to approach it with an open mind, a willingness to engage deeply, and a curiosity about its nuances and complexities. This journey begins by creating the right listening environment. Choose a quiet, comfortable space where you can focus without interruptions. High-quality sound equipment, such as good headphones or speakers, can significantly enhance your listening experience by revealing the intricate details of the music.

Understanding some basic musical concepts and terminology can greatly enhance your enjoyment. Familiarize yourself with elements like melody, harmony, rhythm, and form. Melody is the sequence of notes that you can hum along to; harmony involves the combination of different notes played together to create a richer sound; rhythm is the pattern of beats that gives music its tempo and flow; and form refers to the structure of a piece, such as the sonata, symphony, or concerto. Knowing these basics helps you appreciate the complexity and craftsmanship involved in composing and performing classical music.

Classical music spans several periods, each with its own distinct style and characteristics. The Baroque period (1600-1750) features elaborate musical ornamentation and contrasts, as seen in the works of Johann Sebastian Bach. The Classical period (1750-1820) emphasizes clarity, balance, and form, exemplified by composers like Wolfgang Amadeus Mozart and Ludwig van Beethoven. The Romantic period (1820-1900) focuses on expressive and emotive content, with composers like Johannes Brahms and Richard Wagner creating deeply moving works. Exploring these different periods can provide a broader context and enhance your appreciation for the diversity within classical music.

Active listening is key to truly enjoying classical music. Instead of letting the music fade into the background, focus on the different instruments and how they interact. Pay attention to the dynamics (the variations in loudness and softness), the tempo (the speed of the music), and the thematic development (how melodies and motifs evolve throughout the piece). Notice how composers use contrasts in texture and harmony to create tension and release, guiding your emotional response.

It can be helpful to start with shorter, more accessible pieces and gradually work your way up to longer, more complex compositions. For instance, begin with Beethoven's "Fur Elise" or Bach's "Air on the G String" before tackling Mahler's symphonies or Wagner's operas. Listening to the same piece multiple times can also deepen your appreciation, as repeated hearings often reveal new layers and details that you might have missed initially. Try to identify recurring themes or motifs and see how they are transformed and developed throughout the piece.

Learning about the historical and cultural context of a piece can enhance your listening experience. Read about the composer's life, the era in which they lived, and the circumstances under which the piece was written. Understanding the personal and historical context can add depth to your appreciation and help you connect with the music on a deeper level. Many classical compositions are not just abstract works of art but are deeply intertwined with the personal experiences and historical events of their time.

Attending live performances can significantly enhance your enjoyment of classical music. The experience of hearing a live orchestra or soloist can be profoundly moving and offers a different perspective compared to listening to recordings. Pay attention to the conductor's cues, the musicians' interactions, and the acoustics of the concert hall. The energy and emotion of a live performance can bring the music to life in ways that recordings cannot fully capture. If live performances are not accessible, watching recorded concerts online can also be a valuable experience.

Joining a community of classical music enthusiasts, whether online or in person, can further enrich your experience. Engaging in discussions, sharing your favourite pieces, and learning from others can deepen your understanding and appreciation of the music. Many communities offer resources such as recommended recordings, listening guides, and educational materials that can help you explore classical music more thoroughly.

Experiment with different interpretations of the same piece by various performers or orchestras. Classical music allows for a wide range of interpretive choices, and different performances can highlight different aspects of the music. Comparing interpretations can give you a deeper insight into the nuances of the piece and the artistic decisions made by the performers.

Be open to exploring a wide range of composers and styles. While you might have favourites, stepping out of your comfort zone and listening to unfamiliar works can be very rewarding. Each composer brings their unique voice and perspective, and exploring this diversity can enhance your overall appreciation of classical music. Don't be discouraged if some pieces or composers don't immediately resonate with you; taste in music can evolve over time, and what might seem inaccessible at first can become deeply meaningful with repeated listening and increased familiarity.

Consider using supplementary materials such as program notes, biographies, and historical analyses. Many recordings and live performances include program notes that provide insights into the music's background, structure, and significance. Biographies of composers can offer context about their lives and the influences behind their works. Historical analyses can shed light on the broader cultural and social environment in which the music was created. These resources can enhance your understanding and make the listening experience more engaging.

Finally, approach classical music with a sense of curiosity and exploration. Treat each listening session as an opportunity to discover something new. Be patient with yourself and the music; sometimes it takes time to fully appreciate the depth and complexity of a piece. Allow yourself to be moved by the emotional power of the music, and let it take you on a journey.

Enjoying classical music involves an active and engaged approach. Create an ideal listening environment, familiarize yourself with basic musical concepts, and explore different historical periods and styles. Practice active listening by focusing on the interplay of instruments, dynamics, and thematic development. Repeated listening and exploring different interpretations can deepen your appreciation. Learning about the historical and cultural context of the music can add depth to your experience. Attending live performances and engaging with a community of enthusiasts can further enrich your enjoyment. Approach classical music with curiosity and an open mind, and allow yourself to be transported by its emotional and intellectual richness. With patience and attention, you can cultivate a profound appreciation for the timeless beauty and complexity of classical music.

Don't listen to it while 'working'

Why most of us avoid listening to classical music is because, most of the time we listen to music, while performing some physical activity; such as, dancing, walking, jogging and working out in the gym. Classical music is definitely not the kind of music that will make you tap your feet or make you dance. So, you will have to hear it when you are not undergoing any sort of physical exertion.

Listen to it in the 'Dark'

In contrast to the other popular music genres like pop and hip-hop which gets your adrenaline pumping, classical music is said to have a *soporific*, and a soothing effect. So, hear it when you are in a relaxed frame of mind and not in a commotion. You can listen to classical music either when you are going to sleep or even in the morning, if you rise early. Why? That's because when you are about to sleep or when you get up early, your mind is relatively free and less occupied. That is when classical music will suit your mood and your state of mind.

Listen to the 'Melody'

If you are listening to classical music for the lyrics, then you are not going to listen to it for long. So, what you are supposed to hear in classical music is, its melody. Pay attention to how the music weaves and notes flow. Listen to the variations in rhythm and try identifying the different instruments played in the piece. This will keep you intrigued to the piece you are listening to.

The Music Takes Time to 'Seep in'

It's not a bad thing, if you don't have a liking for classical music. But, if you think that you will be able to like it in one go, after reading this article, then that would be a pretty irrational expectation. When you start any sort of new activity, it will take some time for you to get accustomed to it. It's similar to what happens when you listen to classical music at first. The best way is, when you are alone, working on something or reading a book, let it play in the background. Unconsciously and gradually, classical music will dwell into your mind.

Close your Eyes and Feel

The best way to understand classical music is by closing your eyes and imagining anything that first comes to your mind. You could imagine yourself as performing any activity or if you can't imagine anything and you are blank, then just focus on the music and try to visualize how this music would have been created. Imagine an orchestra playing it and try to figure out all the musical instruments played in the piece.

Every Piece Has a Meaning

Every piece in classical music is meant for a reason. Each piece, though they may have less or no lyrics in them, has a story to narrate. Emotions like anger, love, pain, and beauty are all expressed in the form of variations in music. You will clearly understand it, after you have heard and understood a few pieces.

> *"Classical music is the kind we keep thinking will turn into a tune."*

The above line is such a fantastic quote by *Frank McKinney Hubbard* about classical music. It totally describes how a person who is new to classical music will feel at first. It can feel like a minimalist music piece, but it's more dynamic. Classical music has a broader variety of forms, rhythms and styles. The characteristics of classical music cannot be defined or restricted to a few set of points. Once you have developed an understanding of this music, you will soon be able to enjoy it, whenever you hear it.

While you are doing the above mentioned things, research a little bit about all the classical 'master composers' like Beethoven, Tchaikovsky, Chopin, Mozart, Schoenberg, Haydn, Stravinsky, Schumann, Brahms, Schubert, Handel, Bach, and Debussy. Make a list of their best music pieces and listen to them.

Must-listen-to Classics

I am giving you a 'listening list' of a few of the best classical music pieces, which you can start listening to, and they are as follows:

- Symphony Number 5 - by Beethoven
- Piano concertos 20, 21 - by Mozart
- Carmen - by Bizet
- Rite of Spring - by Stravinsky
- "Pathétique" and "Moonlight" Piano Sonatas - by Beethoven
- "Death and the Maiden" String Quartet - by Schubert
- Brandenburg Concertos - by Bach
- "Pathétique" Symphony - by Tchaikovsky
- Lord Nelson Mass - by Haydn
- Piano Trio No. 1 - by Brahms

It's just like the phenomenon described in the book *'Eat, Pray, Love'*, a bestseller by Elizabeth Gilbert, featuring herself when she is trying to chant a 'mantra' and how she finds it to be annoying and absolutely unlikable. She later understands that the 'Mantra' was affecting her so much because it was changing her and becoming a part of her. I think that is exactly what will happen when you will begin to learn to listen and enjoy classical music. You will initially want to run away from it, but later you will love it, and enjoy it.

CHAPTER 4

A Glimpse Into Hindustani Classical Music

(SHASTRIYA SANGEET)

INDIAN MUSIC IS primarily melodic. Appreciation of it is supposed to be mainly based on the melodic content and rhythm, and not so much on the timbral (the quality of sound that is produced by a particular voice or musical instrument) content. In north Indian classical vocal music (also known as *Hindusthani* vocal music) raga forms the base bone. For each raga there are some distinctive sequences known as *chalans* and *pakads*. A raga is said to elicit some specific emotions from 9 categories referred to in Indian treatises as *Rasas*.

In India, music (*geet*) has been a subject of aesthetic and intellectual discourse since the times of *Vedas (samaveda)*. *Rasa* was examined critically as an essential part of the theory of art by *Bharata* in *Natya Shastra*, (200 century BC). The *rasa* is considered as a state of enhanced emotional perception produced by the presence of musical energy. It is perceived as a sentiment, which could be described as an aesthetic experience. Although unique, one can distinguish several flavors according to the emotion that colors it. Several emotional flavors are listed, namely erotic love (*sringara*), pathetic (*karuna*), devotional (*bhakti*), comic (*hasya*), horrific (*bhayanaka*), repugnant (*bibhatsya*), heroic (*vira*), fantastic, furious (*roudra*), peaceful (*shanta*). Italics represent the corresponding emotion given in the Indian treatises.

Hindustani classical music, also known as Shastriya Sangeet, is one of the two principal forms of Indian classical music, the other being

Carnatic music. This musical tradition has its roots in ancient Vedic rituals, evolving over centuries to become a sophisticated and highly refined art form. Its historical journey spans from the Vedic period through the medieval era, where it absorbed and integrated influences from Persian and Mughal cultures, leading to a unique synthesis of indigenous and foreign musical elements.

The foundation of Hindustani classical music lies in the concept of ragas and talas. A raga is not merely a scale or a mode but a precise combination of notes that evokes a particular mood or sentiment. Each raga has its specific rules, including a set of ascending (arohana) and descending (avarohana) sequences, and characteristic phrases (pakad) that must be adhered to during a performance. Talas, on the other hand, are rhythmic cycles that serve as the structural framework for the music. The interplay between raga and tala allows for a vast scope of improvisation, which is a hallmark of Hindustani classical performances.

The gharana system is another vital aspect of Hindustani music. Gharanas are schools or styles of music, each with its own distinctive approach to the rendition of ragas and talas. They originated from the tradition of master-disciple (guru-shishya) teaching, with knowledge and techniques being passed down through generations. Some of the prominent gharanas include the Gwalior, Agra, Kirana, and Patiala gharanas, each contributing unique styles and techniques to the broader spectrum of Hindustani classical music.

A typical Hindustani classical music performance is characterized by its gradual and deliberate unfolding. It often begins with an alap, an unmetered and improvisational exploration of the raga, which serves to introduce the raga's mood and key motifs. The alap is followed by the jod and jhala, where a rhythmic pulse is introduced and gradually accelerated, leading into the composition (bandish) or song (khayal, dhrupad, etc.). The performance then moves through various improvisational passages, with the musician showcasing their skill in weaving intricate melodic and rhythmic patterns.

The main forms of vocal music in Hindustani classical music include dhrupad, khayal, thumri, and tappa. Dhrupad is the oldest and most austere form, characterized by its solemnity and emphasis on maintaining the purity of the raga. Khayal, which emerged later, is more flexible and allows for greater improvisational freedom, making it the most popular form in contemporary performances. Thumri and tappa are lighter, more lyrical forms, often imbued with romantic and devotional themes.

Instrumentation in Hindustani classical music is diverse and includes both melodic and rhythmic instruments. The sitar, sarod, and bansuri (bamboo flute) are some of the primary melodic instruments, each known for its unique timbre and expressive potential. The tabla, a pair of hand drums, is the most common rhythmic accompaniment, renowned for its intricate patterns and versatility. Other significant instruments include the harmonium, tanpura, and the shehnai.

One of the distinguishing features of Hindustani classical music is its deep connection with spirituality and nature. Many ragas are associated with specific times of the day or seasons, believed to enhance their emotional impact. For instance, the raga Bhairav is traditionally performed in the early morning, while raga Yaman is suited for the evening. This temporal aspect underscores the music's intimate link with the rhythms of life and the natural world.

The patronage of Hindustani classical music has historically been linked to royal courts and temples, where musicians were employed to perform for kings and deities. This patronage played a crucial role in the development and preservation of the art form. In the modern era, the support has extended to cultural institutions, music academies, and festivals, which continue to play a vital role in nurturing and promoting Hindustani classical music.

The 20th century saw the rise of legendary musicians who have left an indelible mark on Hindustani classical music. Figures such as Ustad Allaudin Khan, Pandit Ravi Shankar, Ustad Vilayat Khan, and Ustad Bismillah Khan brought global recognition to the art form. Their virtuosity and innovative approaches not only enriched the tradition but also inspired a new generation of musicians.

Hindustani classical music has also made significant contributions to other genres of music, including film music, jazz, and contemporary classical music. Collaborations between Indian classical musicians and

Western artists have led to exciting new fusions and cross-cultural explorations, expanding the reach and influence of Hindustani music beyond its traditional boundaries.

In the context of pedagogy, the guru-shishya parampara remains the cornerstone of musical training. This ancient method of instruction emphasizes not just the technical aspects of music but also the transmission of cultural and philosophical values. The immersive, one-on-one relationship between the guru and the shishya ensures that the nuances and subtleties of the music are passed down with precision and fidelity.

Despite the challenges posed by modernization and the globalized entertainment industry, Hindustani classical music continues to thrive. Its adaptability, coupled with the dedication of its practitioners and enthusiasts, ensures that this ancient art form remains vibrant and relevant. Concerts, festivals, and music conferences around the world attest to its enduring appeal and the universal resonance of its aesthetic and spiritual dimensions.

In conclusion, Hindustani classical music is not merely a genre of music but a profound cultural expression that encapsulates the historical, spiritual, and artistic heritage of India. Its rich tapestry of ragas, talas, and gharanas, along with its deep-rooted traditions of performance and pedagogy, make it a unique and invaluable part of the world's musical landscape. As it continues to evolve and inspire, Hindustani classical music stands as a testament to the timeless power of art to transcend boundaries and touch the human soul.

Emotions and Indian Classical Music

Indian classical music, encompassing both Hindustani and Carnatic traditions, is deeply intertwined with the expression and evocation of emotions, known as "rasa." The concept of rasa is fundamental to Indian aesthetics and pertains to the essence or flavor that a piece of art, music, or literature evokes in the audience. In Indian classical music, ragas and talas are the primary vehicles through which these emotions are conveyed, creating a profound and transformative experience for both the performer and the listener.

Ragas, the melodic frameworks of Indian classical music, are imbued with specific emotional qualities and are designed to evoke particular states of mind. Each raga is associated with a certain time of day, season, or mood, reflecting the belief that music is intrinsically linked to the natural world and the human psyche. For example, raga Bhairav, often performed in the early morning, evokes a sense of solemnity and devotion, while raga Yaman, typically played in the evening, elicits feelings of peace and romance. This temporal and emotional alignment enhances the listener's experience, making the music a dynamic and immersive art form.

The concept of "rasa" dates back to ancient Indian treatises such as the "Natya Shastra" by Bharata Muni, which identifies nine primary rasas: Shringara (love), Hasya (humor), Karuna (sorrow), Raudra (anger), Veera (heroism), Bhayanaka (fear), Bibhatsa (disgust), Adbhuta (wonder), and Shanta (tranquility). These rasas are not just abstract concepts but are intended to be felt viscerally by the audience. A skilled musician can manipulate the elements of a raga—its notes, intervals, and movements—to elicit these emotions, creating a direct and powerful connection with the listener.

The improvisational nature of Indian classical music plays a crucial role in its emotional expression. Unlike Western classical music, which often relies on written scores, Indian classical music thrives on spontaneity and creativity. During a performance, the musician explores and elaborates on the raga in an extemporaneous manner, allowing for a unique and personal interpretation of its emotional landscape. This improvisation can lead to a deeply intimate and engaging performance, where the musician responds to the mood of the audience and the moment, creating a shared emotional journey.

Talas, the rhythmic cycles in Indian classical music, also contribute significantly to the expression of emotion. The intricate patterns and variations in talas provide a rhythmic framework that supports and enhances the melodic development of the raga. Different talas can evoke different emotional responses; for instance, a fast-paced tala can create excitement and exhilaration, while a slower, more deliberate tala can induce calmness and introspection. The interplay between melody and rhythm is thus essential in shaping the emotional contour of a performance.

Vocal music in Indian classical traditions, particularly in forms such as khayal, dhrupad, and thumri, places a strong emphasis on lyrical expression. The texts of these compositions often explore themes of love, devotion, longing, and nature, allowing the singer to convey complex emotions through both the words and the music. The nuances of vocal techniques, such as ornamentation (gamaka), modulation (meend), and dynamics (layakari), enable the singer to bring out the subtlest shades of emotion, making the performance a rich and emotive experience.

The instrumental music of Indian classical traditions also offers a profound emotional experience, albeit through different means. Instruments like the sitar, sarod, and violin can mimic the human voice's expressive capabilities, using techniques such as gliding between notes (meend) and fast flourishes (taans) to convey emotions. The sensitivity and dexterity required to play these instruments allow musicians to infuse their performances with a wide range of emotional expressions, from the meditative and serene to the passionate and ecstatic.

The guru-shishya (teacher-disciple) tradition in Indian classical music is another crucial factor in the transmission and expression of emotions. This traditional method of teaching emphasizes not just technical proficiency but also the emotional and spiritual dimensions of music. Through close and immersive training, disciples learn to internalize the emotional essence of ragas and compositions, enabling them to convey these emotions authentically in their performances. This deep, personal transmission of knowledge and emotion ensures that the music remains a living and evolving tradition.

The emotional impact of Indian classical music extends beyond the concert stage to spiritual and therapeutic realms. Music has long been considered a path to spiritual enlightenment in Indian culture, with certain ragas and compositions used in meditation and religious rituals. The idea that music can heal and transform is also central to the practice of music therapy, where specific ragas are employed to alleviate stress, anxiety, and other emotional imbalances. The therapeutic use of Indian classical music highlights its profound ability to connect with and affect the human spirit on a deep level.

In modern times, Indian classical music continues to resonate with audiences worldwide, transcending cultural and linguistic barriers. The universal language of emotions that it speaks ensures its relevance and appeal across diverse contexts. Collaborations between Indian classical musicians and artists from various genres, including jazz, Western classical, and contemporary music, have further expanded its emotional reach and expressive possibilities. These cross-cultural exchanges enrich the tradition, bringing new dimensions to its emotional landscape while maintaining its core essence.

Despite the challenges posed by contemporary life, such as the commercialization of music and the influence of digital media, the emotional depth and authenticity of Indian classical music remain its most enduring qualities. The commitment of musicians to preserving and innovating within the tradition ensures that its emotional power continues to be felt by future generations. Festivals, music conferences, and educational initiatives play a vital role in sustaining the tradition, providing platforms for musicians to share their art and connect with audiences.

The relationship between emotions and Indian classical music is profound and multifaceted. Through the intricate interplay of ragas, talas, and improvisation, this music tradition creates an immersive and transformative emotional experience. Whether through the lyrical beauty of vocal performances or the expressive nuances of instrumental music, Indian classical music speaks directly to the heart and soul, making it a timeless and universal form of artistic expression. Its capacity to evoke and communicate deep emotions ensures its place as a treasured and vital part of the world's cultural heritage.

Emotions give meaning to our lives. No aspect of our mental life is more important to the quality and meaning of our existence than emotions. They make life worth living, or sometimes ending. The English word 'emotion' is derived from the French word *émouvoir* which means 'move'. Great classical philosophers—Plato, Aristotle,

Spinoza, Descartes conceived emotion as responses to certain sorts of events triggering bodily changes and typically motivating characteristic behavior. It is difficult to find a consensus on the definition of emotion. Most researchers would probably agree that emotions are relatively brief and intense reactions to goal-relevant changes in the environment that consist of many subcomponents: cognitive appraisal, subjective feeling, physiological arousal, expression, action tendency, and regulation. It therefore suggests that some part of the brain would be selectively activated. Every emotion is associated with autonomic reactions and expressive behaviours. These expressive behaviors or responses to the same stimuli can vary depending on many factors external to the stimuli, like the mood of a person, memory association of the person to the applied stimuli, etc.

The following table based on a wide review of current theories, identifies and contrasts the fundamental emotions according to a set of definite criteria. The three key criteria used include:

1. Mental experiences that have a strongly motivating subjective quality like pleasure or pain;
2. Mental experiences that are in response to some event or object that is either real or imagined;
3. Mental experiences that motivate particular kinds of behaviour. The combination of these attributes distinguish the emotions from sensations, feelings and moods.

Kind of Emotion	Positive Emotions	Negative Emotions
Related to object properties	Interest, curiosity	Alarm, panic
	Attraction, desire, admiration	Aversion, disgust, revulsion
	Surprise, amusement	Indifference, familiarity, habituation
Future appraisal	Hope	Fear

Event related	Gratitude, thankfulness	Anger, rage
	Joy, elation, triumph, jubilation	Sorrow, grief
	Relief	Frustration, disappointment
Self-appraisal	Pride in achievement, self-confidence, sociability	Embarrassment, shame, guilt, remorse
Social	Generosity	Avarice, greed, miserliness, envy, jealousy
Catheter	Sympathy	Cruelty

While sound stimuli may cause general physiological changes ("arousal"), these changes must be interpreted cognitively in order for a specific emotion to emerge. The listener does not come to the listening experience as a blank slate. He or she already has existing musically pertinent knowledge. Even for a musically untrained listener the general exposure to listening to music since childhood is also learning, though not formal.

Thus any emotional behavior, even habitual and seemingly automatic and natural, is actually learned. In case of music this behavior serves as a means of communication, since often emotional behavior is differentiable and intelligible. One major problem that arises in the study of the emotional power of music is that the emotional content of music is very subjective. A piece of music may be undeniably emotionally powerful, and at the same time be experienced in very different ways by each person who hears it. The emotion created by a piece of music may be affected by memories associated with the piece, by the environment it is being played in, by the mood of the person listening and their personality, by the culture they were brought up in; by any number of factors both impossible to control and impossible to quantify. Under such circumstances, it is extremely difficult to deduce what intrinsic quality of the music, if any, created a specific emotional response in the listener.

The individual feels immersed in that mood to the exclusion of anything else including himself. It may be noted that during the musical experience, the mind experiences conscious joy even in the representation of painful events because of the integration of perceptual, emotional, and cognitive faculties in a more expanded and enhanced auditory perception, completed by the subtle aesthetic of sensing, feeling, understanding and hearing all at the same time. The Eastern approach to emotional aesthetics and intelligence treats *rasa* as a multi-dimensional principle that explains thoroughly the relation between a sentiment, a mood, the creative process and its transpersonal qualities. This transpersonal domain includes the super-conscious or spiritual state and therefore acts as an interface between individual and collective unconscious states.

Rasa conveys the idea of an aesthetic beauty knowable only through the feeling. This aesthetic experience is a transformation of not merely feeling, but equally of cognition, a comprehensive understanding in the mode of ecstasy of the intellect, itself inscrutable and illuminating. In the Vedas the experience of *rasa* is described as a flash of inner consciousness, which appears to whom the knowledge of ideal beauty is innate and intuitive.

Rasa is not the unique property of the art itself. It unites the art with the creator and the observer in the same state of consciousness, and requires the power of imagination and representation and therefore a kind of intellectual sensibility.

Emotional attributes of notes

Indian music is known for its complex use of microtones (*shruti*). But for notation and explanation, it has been divide an octave into 12 semitones. We use a movable scale, which means it can be started from anywhere. The starting point is the root of the octave (*saptak*), all the other notes are defined in relation to the root of the octave. Each of the 12 notes in the octave has a unique identity, given by S, r, R, g, G, m, M, P, d, D, n, N.

The chromatic scale in Hindustani Classical Music

Note name	Notation ID	Sol-fa syllable	Full name	Western equivalent
Sa	S	sa	Shadaja	Unison
Re (*komal*)	r	re	Rishabha (*komal*)	Minor second
Re (*shuddha*)	R	re	Rishabha (*shuddha*)	Major second
Ga (*komal*)	g	ga	Gandhara (*komal*)	Minor third
Ga (*shuddha*)	G	ga	Gandhara (*shuddha*)	Major third
Ma (*shuddha*)	m	ma	Madhyama (*shuddha*)	Perfect fourth
Ma (*teevra*)	M	ma	Madhyama (*teevra*)	Augmented fourth
Pa	P	pa	Panchama	Perfect fifth
Dha (*komal*)	d	dha	Dhaivata (*komal*)	Minor sixth
Dha (*shuddha*)	D	dha	Dhaivata (*shuddha*)	Major sixth
Ni (*komal*)	n	ni	Nishada (*komal*)	Minor seventh
Ni (*shuddha*)	N	ni	Nishada (*shuddha*)	Major seventh
Sa	S'	Sa'	Shadaja	Octave

Shadja like a *yogi* beyond any attachment

Rishabha (komala) rather sluggish

Rishabha (shuddha) reminding of indolence of a person waking up from sleep

Gandhara (komala) bewildered, helpless and pitiable

Gandhara (shuddha) fresh and pleasant

Madhyama (shuddha) grave, noble and powerful

Madhyama (teevra) sensitive, luxurious

Panchama brilliant, self-composing

Dhaivata (komala) grief, pathos

Dhaivata (shuddha) robust, lustful

Nishada (komala) gentle, happy, affectionate

Nishada (shuddha) piercing appeal

However, *Bharata* agrees that only four *rasas*, namely *Karuna, Shanta, Shringara* and *Vira* may actually be experienced from a single note. He further proposes that when *Shuddha madhyama* dominates a melody, it creates a serene and sublime atmosphere, while a dominant *Panchama* creates an invigorating and erotic feeling. Pandit Vishnu Narayana Bhatkhande in his work suggested the inadequacy of *vadi svara* (i.e. the main melodic tone of the raga) in determining the *rasa* of ragas. However, he mentions that *Ragas* employing *Shuddha* (*Rishabha, Dhaivata* and *Gandhara*) emote *Shringara rasa*, and those employing *Komala* (*Dhaivata* and *Nishad*) emote *Vira rasa*. This view is contradicted because an individual note cannot produce emotion, and they may do so only in a specific context. This implies that expression is born by the melodic content.

Of the eight emotions listed in the opinion score sheets, only six represent *rasas*. These are Heroic (*Vira*), Anger (*Raudra*), Serenity (*Shanta*), Devotion (*Bhakti*), Sorrow (*Karuna*), Romantic (*Shringara*). Other two emotions namely Joy and Anxiety have been considered additionally.

Given below some selected *ragas* and their corresponding *rasas*:

Ragas	*Rasas*
Adana	Vira
Bhairav	Raudra, Shanta, Bhakti, Karuna
Chayanat	Shringara
Darbari Kanhara	Shanta
Hindol	Vira, Raudra
Jayjayvanti	Shringara
Jogiya	Karuna, Shringara, Bhakti
Kedar	Shanta
Mian-ki-Malhar	Karuna
Mian-ki-Todi	Bhakti, Shrigara, Karuna
Shree	Shanta

There are seven pure notes, namely: *Sa* (Do), *Re* (Re), *Ga* (Mi), *Ma* (Fa), *Pa* (Sol), *Dha* (La), and *Ni* (Si). The five altered notes are re, ga, Ma, dha, and ni; in which re, ga, dha, and ni are flat, and Ma is sharp. In the result section, notes in sequences were denoted by the first letter of each of the aforesaid notes. The abbreviated sequence of notes used therein are S, r, R, g, G, m, M, P, d, D, n, and N.

Relationship between note sequences and emotion in Indian *Ragas*:

Note Sequence	Major emotional Response
mSN	Anger, Devotion, Anxiety
RgM	Heroic, Anxiety
SgR	Heroic, Romantic
GMmP	Romantic, Serenity, Anxiety
Pmd	Heroic, Anxiety, Sorrow
SND	Anger, Devotion
DPmP	Romantic, Serenity
rGrS	Heroic, Devotion, Anxiety
GMR	Devotion
MGR	Devotion
NDP	Heroic, Anxiety, Sorrow
NDm	Anger
mPmG	Heroic, Devotion, Anxiety
mGr	Heroic, Devotion, Anxiety
dPMG	Heroic, Anxiety, Sorrow
grS	Heroic, Devotion
PmG	Heroic, Devotion, Anxiety
RGM	Devotion
gRS	Romantic, Serenity
GMP	Anxiety
DPm	Romantic, Serenity
MdP	Heroic, Anxiety, Sorrow
MPdP	Heroic, Anxiety, Sorrow
GrS	Heroic, Devotion, Anxiety
PMGM	Anxiety
MPd	Heroic, Anxiety, Sorrow
NSR	Devotion
PMG	Devotion
dPM	Anxiety

As we can see, short sequences of 3-4 notes, specific for ragas, can evoke particular emotions.

There is the subject of preventive medicine and curative medicine. Likewise there is also remedial music. It comprises of music and musical compositions that can be listened to for a short time every day. This ensures sound health. Every night before retiring to bed, one can listen to soft music played on a string instrument or he/she can herself play the instrument if he/she/knows to play. *Ragas* have a soothing effect on the nerves. This listener will not only have a sound sleep, but will also improve the power of immunity against attacks of diseases. Music therapy is a good tranquilizer in these days of anxiety, stress, tension and high pressure living. It can be given along with the other systems of medication/treatment. Empty stomach is not conducive to music therapy and should be avoided. The best times for music therapy treatment are morning, evening and night. Short sessions of 20 minutes duration with an interval of 15 minutes may be resorted to in music therapy. Two or three sessions are advisable at a stretch. Relaxing or soothing music can be played during labour pains. In South India, there is a tradition, which pregnant women who listen to the sweet music of *Veena* are assured of safe delivery. It is said that the first sense that develops in a child in the womb is the "hearing sense" and the harmonic music emanating from the strings of *Veena* – the divine instrument penetrates the womb and makes the child feel the divine soothing effect. Music from strings has the capacity to penetrate the skin. Music on *Veena* is said to be very effective since the structure of *Veena* is very much identical to the structure of a human body. There are many resemblances between the human body (*Daiva Veena*) and man-made *Veena*.

Just mentioning a few similarities here to prove the point that music from *Veena* is nothing but truly divine. *Veena* has 24 frets, 4 strings on the frets and 3 on the side (they are the *tala* strings). The four strings represent the *Chatur Veda- Rig, Yajur, Sama* and *Athharva*. The 24 frets represents 12 *swarasthanas* in two octaves (24). Just like the 24 frets of the *Veena*, human back bone has 24 divisions. According to the anatomy, the back bone has 7 cervices, 12 thoracic and 5 lumbar vertebras. In Veena the distance between each fret is broad in the lower octaves and becomes less while proceeding towards the higher octaves. Similarly the back bone is thick at the *Mooladhara* (seat point of human back bone) and the distance between each ring becomes less while proceeding towards the back of the neck. The *nadis Ida* and *Pingla* in the human body represents the strings. All *swaras* have the variations except S and P. Sa referred as *Adhara Shadja* is constant, stable and this note *Shadja* represents the eternal divine power and source of wisdom and knowledge which is the base of all music in the world. The human body which resembles a *Veena* emanates *Nada* through the *Nabhi* (naval), *Hridaya* (heart), *Kantha* (throat), Tongue and Nose (represented by *Shira* -Head). Every human being has music in them. Some are able to sing while some others are not. It doesn't mean that those who are not able to sing, doesn't have music in them. The inherent talent of music has to be cultivated just like we dig the earth for water. As we keep on digging slowly the flow of water deep inside can be seen. Further efforts bring out the water like a spring of river. It is the same case with music. (The relation between *Veena* and Human Body is itself a very exhaustive topic and shall be dealt with in a dissertation manner).

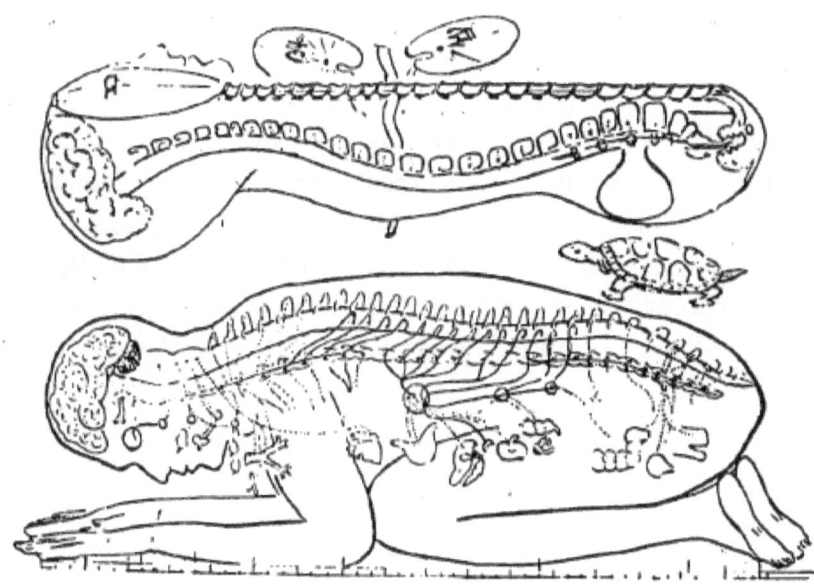

The importance of various *chakras* in spiritual path is well known. In the following figure the production of various *beeja mantras* (seed-sounds) in relation to various chakras starting from *Mooladhara* at the base are shown.

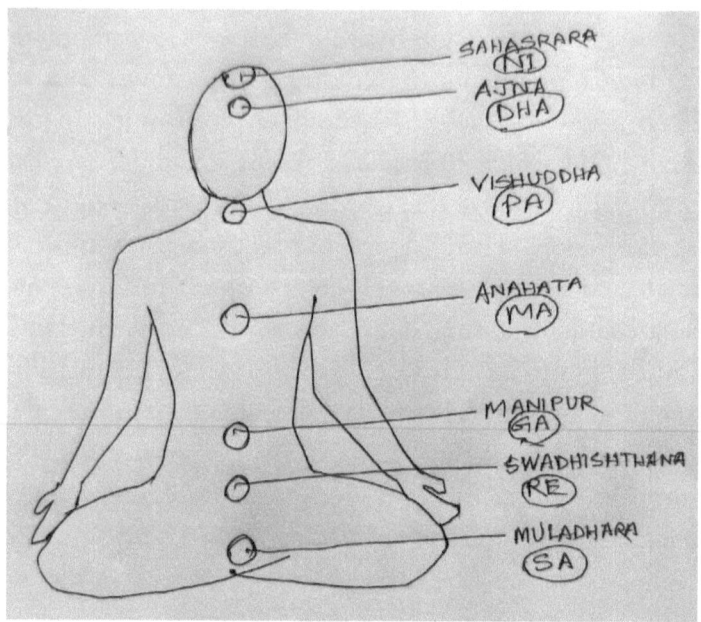

The Vedic representation of the human spinal cord as the musical instrument (*Veena*) is shown in the other following figure. The 24 frets of the instrument are analogous to the 24 cartilages in the spinal cord. The number 24 also relates to the 24 syllables in the Vedic *Gayatri mantra*. Thus the inter-relation between the production of seed-sounds at the various chakras in the spinal cord and representation of *Veena* as spinal cord shows the multi-faceted manifestations of Vedic principles and experiences.

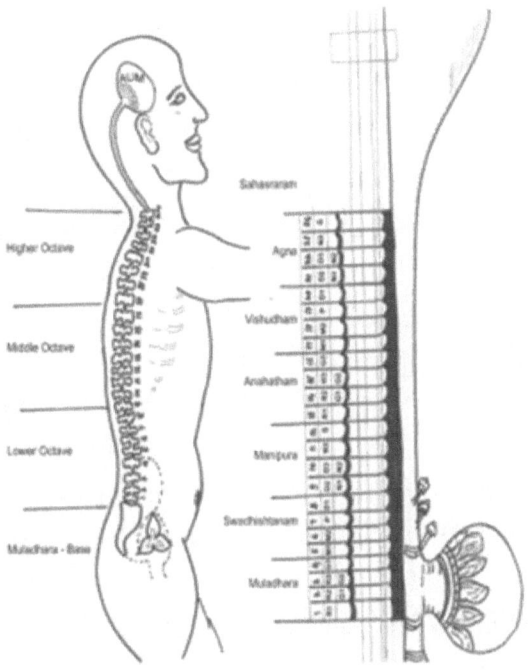

Coming back to the topic under discussion, quiet listening of music under relaxed conditions is absolutely essential. The patient can lie down on an easy chair or a cot completely relaxed. Ragas to cure Sleeping Disorders Certain Ragas like Neelambari, Anandabhairavi, Kalyani etc. has been found very effective for sleep disorders. Sleep disorders may result in fatigue, tiredness, depression and problems in daytime functioning. Music results in decreased anxiety, blood pressure, heart and respiratory rate and may have positive effects on sleep via muscle relaxation and distraction from thoughts.

CHAPTER: 5

'Chakras' And 'Ragas'

THE CONNECTION BETWEEN chakras, the energy centres within the body according to Hindu and yogic traditions, and ragas, the melodic frameworks of Indian classical music, is a fascinating exploration of the intersection between spirituality, physiology, and art. In traditional Indian philosophy, the human body is believed to be composed of seven main chakras, each associated with specific physical, emotional, and spiritual qualities. These chakras are thought to be aligned along the spinal column, from the base of the spine to the crown of the head, with each chakra corresponding to a particular frequency of energy vibration.

Similarly, ragas in Indian classical music are also associated with specific emotional and psychological states, as well as with particular times of day, seasons, and natural elements. Each raga is believed to evoke a distinct mood or sentiment, ranging from joy and serenity to longing and melancholy. The intricate combination of notes, intervals, and rhythmic patterns within a raga is thought to resonate with the subtle energy centres of the body, stimulating and harmonizing the corresponding chakras.

The relationship between chakras and ragas can be understood through the concept of resonance—the idea that certain frequencies of sound can influence and affect the vibrational patterns of the body and mind. According to this view, when a musician performs a raga, the specific frequencies produced by the music resonate with the energy centres of the listener, activating and balancing the corresponding chakras. For example, a raga associated with the heart chakra (Anahata) may evoke feelings of love, compassion, and emotional openness, while also facilitating the release of blockages or imbalances in this area.

Each chakra is believed to be associated with specific musical elements, such as pitch, tempo, and dynamics, which correspond to the qualities of the corresponding raga. For instance, the root chakra (Muladhara), located at the base of the spine, is associated with stability, grounding, and physical vitality, qualities that may be reflected in the deep, resonant tones and steady rhythms of ragas performed in lower registers. In contrast, the crown chakra (Sahasrara), located at the top of the head, is associated with spiritual awakening, transcendence, and universal consciousness, qualities that may be reflected in the ethereal melodies and expansive rhythms of ragas performed in higher registers.

The practice of raga therapy, a form of sound healing rooted in Indian classical music, seeks to harness the therapeutic potential of ragas to promote physical, emotional, and spiritual well-being. By selecting ragas that correspond to specific chakras or healing intentions, practitioners aim to balance and harmonize the energy centres of the body, promoting relaxation, stress relief, and inner transformation. This approach is often used in conjunction with other holistic therapies, such as yoga, meditation, and Ayurveda, to support overall health and wellness.

In addition to its therapeutic applications, the connection between chakras and ragas has profound implications for the practice and appreciation of Indian classical music. By understanding the emotional, psychological, and spiritual dimensions of ragas in relation to the chakra system, musicians and listeners alike can deepen their understanding and experience of the music. The performance of ragas can thus be seen not only as a form of artistic expression but also as a means of self-discovery, healing, and spiritual awakening.

Furthermore, the exploration of chakras and ragas highlights the interconnectedness of different cultural and philosophical traditions, illustrating how ancient wisdom and modern science can converge in their understanding of the human experience. As interest in holistic and integrative approaches to health and wellness continues to grow, the relationship between chakras and ragas offers a rich and fertile ground for exploration and discovery, bridging the gap between art and science, tradition and innovation, East and West. Through the practice and appreciation of Indian classical music, we can tap into the transformative power of sound to nourish the body, mind, and spirit, and to awaken to the fullness of our potential as human beings.

Hindustani classical music is based upon *ragas* and *taalas*, each designed to affect different *"chakras"* (energy centers, or "moods") in the path of the *'Kundalini'*. Vedic practice traces specific physical, Mental, Biological and spiritual results associated with activation of these centers. Indian classical music has one of the most complicated and complete musical systems ever developed. It has the same aspects of Western classical music, as the 8 basic notes (*Sa, Re, Ga, Ma, Pa, Dha, Ni, Sa'*), in order.

Raaga, in the Sanskrit dictionary, is defined as 'the act of coloring or dyeing' (the mind in this context) and 'any feeling or passion especially love, affection, sympathy, vehement desire, interest, joy, or delight'. In music, these descriptions apply to the impressions of melodic sounds on both the artist(s) and listener(s). A *raaga* consists of required and optional rules governing the melodic movements of notes within a performance. The rules of a *raaga* can be defined by the manner in which the notes are used, i.e. specific ways of ornamenting notes or emphasizing/de-emphasizing them, manner in which the scale is ascended or descended Optional or required musical phrases, the way in which to reveal these phrases, and/or combine them, the octave or frequency range to emphasize The relative pacing between the notes The time of day and/or season when the *raaga* may be performed so as to invoke the emotions of the *raaga* for maximum impact on the mental and emotional state of the performer and listener.

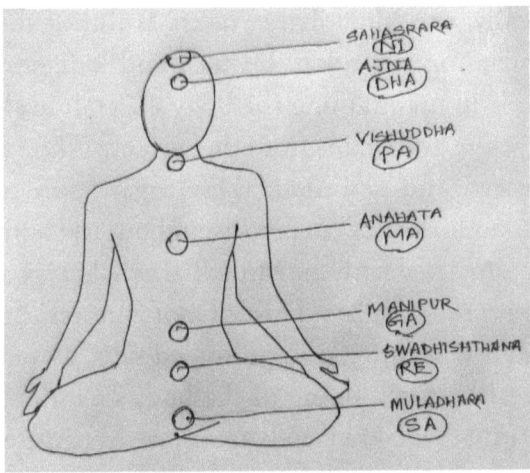

FIRST CHAKRA: *Muladhara*: Earth Security & Survival.
Location: The end of the spine between the anus and the sexual organs.
Organ/Gland: Organs of elimination.
Colour: Red.
Qualities: Grounded, centered, secure, loyal and stable which is responsible for healthy functions of elimination.
Shadow: Fear, insecurity. Life feels like a burden; feeling of not really belonging on earth or in one's culture or family. Weak constitution, elimination problems, reduced physical and mental resistance, sexual perversions.
Yoga exercises: Crow Pose, Chair Pose, Body drops, Frog Pose, *Mulbhandh*, Front stretches, lying on the stomach, feet kicking buttocks.

The Muladhara chakra, the first of the seven main energy centers in the body according to Hindu and yogic traditions, is situated at the base of the spine, between the anus and the sexual organs. It is associated with the element of earth and is often referred to as the root chakra, as it serves as the foundation upon which our physical and emotional well-being is built. The Muladhara chakra governs our sense of security, stability, and survival instincts, providing us with a deep-rooted sense of grounded-ness and belonging in the world.

Physiologically, the Muladhara chakra is linked to the organs of elimination, including the colon, bladder, and kidneys. These organs play a crucial role in maintaining the body's overall health and vitality by eliminating waste and toxins from the system. When the Muladhara chakra is balanced and activated, these organs function optimally, ensuring the smooth flow of energy throughout the body.

The colour associated with the Muladhara chakra is red, symbolizing vitality, strength, and vitality. This vibrant hue reflects the chakra's qualities of stability, security, and grounded-ness, as well as its role in ensuring the healthy functioning of the body's elimination processes. When the Muladhara chakra is in balance, we feel grounded, centered, and secure in ourselves and our surroundings, with a strong sense of loyalty and stability in our relationships and endeavours.

However, when the Muladhara chakra is blocked or imbalanced, we may experience a range of physical, emotional, and psychological symptoms. These can include feelings of fear, insecurity, and instability, as well as a sense of disconnection from our roots and a lack of belonging in the world. Physically, imbalances in the Muladhara chakra may manifest as weak constitution, elimination problems, reduced physical and mental resistance, and sexual perversions.

To balance and activate the Muladhara chakra, various yoga exercises and poses can be practiced. These include poses that focus on grounding and stability, such as the Crow Pose, Chair Pose, and Frog Pose, as well as exercises that engage the muscles of the pelvic floor, such as Mulbhandh and Front Stretches. Lying on the stomach and performing feet kicking buttocks exercises can also help to stimulate and activate the Muladhara chakra, promoting a sense of rootedness and stability in the body and mind.

In summary, the Muladhara chakra is the foundation of our physical and emotional well-being, providing us with a sense of security, stability, and belonging in the world. When balanced and activated, it ensures the healthy functioning of our elimination organs and promotes a deep-rooted sense of grounded ness and loyalty. Through yoga practices and mindful awareness, we can nurture and support the Muladhara chakra, fostering a sense of security and stability that allows us to thrive in all aspects of our lives.

SECOND CHAKRA: *Swadhisthana:* Water Creativity.
Location: The sexual organs.
Organ/Gland: Sexual organs, reproductive glands, kidneys, bladder.
Colour: Orange.
Qualities: Positive, relaxed attitude to sexual functions; patience; creativity; responsible relationships.
Shadow: Rigid emotions, frigidity, guilt, no boundaries, irresponsible relationships. Problems with reproductive organs, or kidneys.
Yoga exercises: Frog Pose, Cobra Pose, Butterfly, *Sat Kriya*, Cat-Cow, *Maha Mudra*,
Pelvic Lifts.

The Swadhisthana chakra, often referred to as the sacral chakra, is the second of the seven main energy centres in the body according to Hindu and yogic traditions. Located in the lower abdomen, specifically at the level of the sexual organs, the Swadhisthana chakra is associated with the element of water and is responsible for our creativity, emotional well-being, and sexuality. This chakra governs our ability to experience pleasure, form healthy relationships, and cultivate a positive attitude towards our sexual and creative impulses.

Physiologically, the Swadhisthana chakra is connected to the sexual organs, reproductive glands, kidneys, and bladder. These organs play a vital role in our reproductive health and urinary function, as well as in the regulation of our sexual energy. When the Swadhisthana chakra is balanced and activated, these organs function optimally, supporting our overall well-being and vitality.

The colour associated with the Swadhisthana chakra is orange, symbolizing warmth, creativity, and vitality. This vibrant hue reflects the chakra's qualities of creativity, emotional expression, and sensuality, as well as its role in nurturing responsible and fulfilling relationships. When the Swadhisthana chakra is in balance, we feel emotionally stable, creatively inspired, and capable of forming intimate connections with others based on trust, respect, and mutual understanding.

However, when the Swadhisthana chakra is blocked or imbalanced, we may experience a range of physical, emotional, and psychological symptoms. These can include rigid emotions, feelings of guilt or shame surrounding sexuality, difficulty in forming healthy boundaries in relationships, and problems with reproductive organs or urinary function.

To balance and activate the Swadhisthana chakra, various yoga exercises and poses can be practiced. These include poses that focus on opening and energizing the pelvic region, such as Frog Pose, Cobra Pose, and Butterfly Pose, as well as exercises that engage the muscles of the abdomen and lower back, such as Cat-Cow and Pelvic Lifts. Sat Kriya and Maha Mudra are also beneficial practices for stimulating the flow of energy through the sacral chakra, promoting creativity, emotional well-being, and healthy sexuality.

In summary, the Swadhisthana chakra is the centre of our creativity, emotional expression, and sexuality, governing our ability to experience pleasure, form healthy relationships, and cultivate a positive attitude towards our bodies and desires. When balanced and activated, it allows us to embrace our creative impulses, express our emotions authentically, and engage in fulfilling and responsible relationships. Through yoga practices and mindful awareness, we can nurture and support the Swadhisthana chakra, fostering a sense of creativity, emotional well-being, and vitality that enriches every aspect of our lives.

THIRD CHAKRA: *Manipura:* Fire Action & Balance.
Location: The area of the Navel Point, solar plexus.
Organ/Gland: Navel plexus, liver, gall bladder, spleen, digestive organs, pancreas, adrenals
Colour: Yellow.
Qualities: The center of personal power and commitment. Self-esteem, identity, judgment. This is where the strength for inner balance, inspiration and good health is developed.

Shadow: Anger; greed, shame, despair. Obstacles everywhere. Not enough strength and spontaneity. Conforming in order to be recognized. Refuting one's own wishes and emotions. Problems with digestion, the liver, the gallbladder, and the pancreas.
Yoga exercises: Stretch Pose, Sat Kriya, Peacock Pose, Bow Pose, Fish Pose, Diaphram Lock, Breath of Fire; all exercises which train the abdominal muscles.

The Manipura chakra, also known as the solar plexus chakra, is the third of the seven main energy centres in the body according to Hindu and yogic traditions. Situated in the area of the navel point, or solar plexus, the Manipura chakra is associated with the element of fire and is responsible for our sense of personal power, willpower, and self-esteem. This chakra governs our ability to take action, make decisions, and maintain inner balance in the face of life's challenges.

Physiologically, the Manipura chakra is connected to the navel plexus, as well as organs such as the liver, gall bladder, spleen, digestive organs, pancreas, and adrenal glands. These organs play a crucial role in our digestion, metabolism, and energy regulation, as well as in the production of hormones that govern our stress response and emotional well-being. When the Manipura chakra is balanced and activated, these organs function optimally, supporting our overall health and vitality.

The colour associated with the Manipura chakra is yellow, symbolizing warmth, vitality, and energy. This vibrant hue reflects the chakra's qualities of personal power, self-esteem, and inner strength, as well as its role in fostering confidence, courage, and clarity of purpose. When the Manipura chakra is in balance, we feel empowered, confident, and capable of taking decisive action to achieve our goals and aspirations.

However, when the Manipura chakra is blocked or imbalanced, we may experience a range of physical, emotional, and psychological symptoms. These can include feelings of anger, frustration, or resentment, as well as issues related to self-esteem, identity, and judgment. Physically, imbalances in the Manipura chakra may manifest as digestive problems, liver disorders, gallbladder issues, or adrenal fatigue.

To balance and activate the Manipura chakra, various yoga exercises and poses can be practiced. These include poses that focus on strengthening and energizing the abdominal muscles, such as the Stretch Pose, Peacock Pose, Bow Pose, and Fish Pose, as well as exercises that engage the diaphragm and promote deep, rhythmic breathing, such as Sat Kriya and Breath of Fire. These practices help to stimulate the flow of energy through the solar plexus chakra, promoting a sense of inner balance, inspiration, and good health.

In summary, the Manipura chakra is the centre of our personal power and commitment, governing our ability to take action, make decisions, and maintain inner balance in the face of life's challenges. When balanced and activated, it allows us to tap into our inner strength, courage, and confidence, empowering us to pursue our goals and aspirations with clarity and determination. Through yoga practices and mindful awareness, we can nurture and support the Manipura chakra, fostering a sense of vitality, resilience, and self-assurance that enables us to thrive in all aspects of our lives.

FOURTH CHAKRA: *Anahata:* Air Balance Point: Love & Compassion
Location: The middle of the chest on the breast bone at the level of the nipples.
Organ/Gland: Heart, lungs, thymus gland.
Colour: Green.
Qualities: Compassion; kindness; forgiveness; service; love. Recognizing and understandingthese qualities in others. Sacred transformation. Awakening to spiritual awareness.
Shadow: Grief. Attachment. Closed to surroundings. Easily hurt. Dependent on love and affection from others. Fear of rejection. Helper syndrome. Heartlessness. Heart problems; lung problems; blood pressure problems.
Yoga exercises: Ego Eradicator, Yoga Mudra, Bear Grip, Baby Pose (strengthens the heart muscles). All arm exercises, and exercises which twist the upper torso. All *Pranayam*.

The Anahata chakra, commonly known as the heart chakra, stands as the fourth of the seven primary energy centres within the body, as per the ancient traditions of Hinduism and yoga. Positioned at the midpoint of the chest, aligned with the breastbone and the level of the nipples, this chakra is linked with the element of air and is revered as the focal point of love, compassion, and emotional balance. The Anahata chakra orchestrates our capacity to experience and express profound emotions, fostering qualities such as empathy, kindness, forgiveness, and service towards others, epitomizing the essence of unconditional love.

Physiologically, the Anahata chakra is intricately connected with the heart, lungs, and the thymus gland. These vital organs are integral to our respiratory and circulatory systems, regulating the flow of oxygen-rich blood throughout the body and nurturing our physical well-being. When the Anahata chakra is harmoniously balanced and activated, these organs function optimally, facilitating not only physical vitality but also emotional equilibrium and spiritual awakening.

The colour associated with the Anahata chakra is green, symbolizing growth, harmony, and renewal. This verdant hue mirrors the chakra's qualities of compassion, healing, and sacred transformation, serving as a beacon for our journey towards spiritual awareness and enlightenment. When the Anahata chakra is awakened, we are able to recognize and understand these qualities not only within ourselves but also in others, fostering deep connections and nurturing relationships that transcend ego and self-interest.

However, when the Anahata chakra is blocked or imbalanced, we may encounter a myriad of physical, emotional, and psychological challenges. These may include feelings of grief, attachment, and emotional pain, as well as difficulties in forming meaningful connections, and a sense of being closed off to the world around us. Physically, imbalances in the Anahata chakra may manifest as heart problems, lung disorders, or issues with blood pressure, reflecting the interconnectedness between our emotional and physical well-being.

To balance and activate the Anahata chakra, a variety of yoga exercises and practices can be incorporated into our daily routines. These may include techniques such as Ego Eradicator, Yoga Mudra, Bear

Grip, and Baby Pose, all of which serve to strengthen the heart muscles and promote flexibility in the chest and upper torso. Additionally, arm exercises and movements that involve twisting the upper body can help to release tension and energy blockages within the Anahata chakra, facilitating a sense of openness, receptivity, and emotional release. Pranayama, or yogic breathing exercises, are also highly beneficial for harmonizing and energizing the heart chakra, promoting a sense of inner peace, balance, and spiritual connection.

In summary, the Anahata chakra serves as the gateway to love, compassion, and spiritual awakening, guiding us towards a deeper understanding of ourselves and the world around us. When balanced and activated, it enables us to cultivate qualities such as kindness, forgiveness, and service, fostering connections that transcend ego and self-interest. Through yoga practices and mindful awareness, we can nurture and support the Anahata chakra, awakening to the transformative power of love and compassion, and embracing a path of healing, wholeness, and spiritual evolution.

FIFTH CHAKRA: *Vishuddha:* Ether: Projective Power of the Word
Location: The throat.
Organ/Gland: Trachea, throat, cervical vertebrae, thyroid.
Colour: Light blue.
Qualities: The center for truth, language, knowledge and the ability to communicate
effectively. Authenticity. Healthy self-expression and interactions. Inspiring, teaching.
Embodying God's Will.
Shadow: Lethargy, weakness in expressive and descriptive abilities. Shyness, voice problems, insecurity, fear of other people's opinions and judgments.
Throat problems, neck problems, thyroid problems.
Yoga exercises: All Chanting. Shoulder Stand, Cobra Pose, Plow Pose, Camel Pose, Cat-Cow, Neck Rolls, Neck Lock, nose to knees.

The Vishuddha chakra, situated at the throat, represents the fifth of the seven main energy centres in the body according to Hindu and yogic traditions. Referred to as the throat chakra, it embodies the element of ether and serves as the conduit for the projective power of the spoken word. This chakra is the locus of truth, language, knowledge, and the ability to communicate effectively, facilitating authentic self-expression, healthy interactions, and the embodiment of divine will.

Physiologically, the Vishuddha chakra is closely linked with the trachea, throat, cervical vertebrae, and the thyroid gland. These structures play pivotal roles in our respiratory system, vocalization, and hormonal regulation, influencing both our physical health and our ability to express ourselves verbally and authentically. When the Vishuddha chakra is balanced and activated, these organs function optimally, enabling us to articulate our thoughts and feelings with clarity, confidence, and integrity.

The colour associated with the Vishuddha chakra is light blue, symbolizing clarity, purity, and serenity. This tranquil hue reflects the chakra's qualities of truthfulness, authenticity, and self-expression, serving as a beacon for our journey towards embodying our true selves and communicating our innermost truths to the world. When the Vishuddha chakra is awakened, we are able to express ourselves freely and confidently, inspiring and teaching others with our words and actions.

However, when the Vishuddha chakra is blocked or imbalanced, we may experience a range of physical, emotional, and psychological symptoms. These may include feelings of lethargy, weakness, or insecurity in our expressive abilities, as well as shyness, fear of judgment, and difficulty in asserting ourselves or speaking our truth. Physically, imbalances in the Vishuddha chakra may manifest as throat problems, neck tension, or thyroid disorders, reflecting the interconnectedness between our inner state and our physical health.

To balance and activate the Vishuddha chakra, a variety of yoga exercises and practices can be employed. These may include techniques such as chanting, which helps to resonate the vocal cords and energize the throat chakra, as well as asanas (poses) that focus on stretching and strengthening the neck and throat muscles, such as Shoulder Stand, Cobra Pose, Plow Pose, Camel Pose, Cat-Cow, Neck Rolls, Neck Lock, and nose to knees. These practices help to release tension and energy blockages within the Vishuddha chakra, facilitating clear communication, authentic self-expression, and a sense of inner harmony and alignment.

In summary, the Vishuddha chakra serves as the gateway to truth, knowledge, and effective communication, empowering us to express ourselves authentically and embody our divine purpose. When balanced and activated, it enables us to speak our truth with confidence, clarity, and integrity, inspiring and teaching others with our words and actions. Through yoga practices and mindful awareness, we can nurture and support the Vishuddha chakra, awakening to the transformative power of authentic self-expression and embodying our highest potential as beings of light and wisdom.

SIXTH CHAKRA: *Ajna:* The Third Eye. Intuition, Wisdom & Identity
Location: Between the eyebrows.
Organ/Gland: Brain; pituitary gland.
Colour: Indigo.
Qualities: Center of intuition, clairvoyance; visualizing; fantasizing; concentration and
determination. Self-initiation. Power of projection. Understanding your purpose.
Shadow: Confusion, depression. Rejection of spirituality. Over-intellectualizing.
Yoga exercises: Meditating on the Third Eye, Long Chant, *Kirtan Kriya*. Archer Pose.

Whistle Breaths. Yoga Mudra. All exercises where the forehead rests on the floor.

The Ajna chakra, often referred to as the Third Eye, stands as the sixth of the seven main energy centres within the body according to Hindu and yogic traditions. Positioned between the eyebrows, this chakra embodies the element of light and serves as the focal point for intuition, wisdom, and the exploration of one's true identity. The Ajna chakra is the seat of inner knowing, clairvoyance, and visualization, facilitating deep concentration, determination, and self-initiation on the spiritual path.

Physiologically, the Ajna chakra is closely associated with the brain and the pituitary gland, often referred to as the master gland of the endocrine system. These structures play pivotal roles in regulating our thoughts, emotions, and bodily functions, as well as in facilitating our perception of the world around us. When the Ajna chakra is balanced and activated, our intuitive faculties are sharpened, allowing us to tap into higher states of consciousness and gain insights into our true purpose and identity.

The colour associated with the Ajna chakra is indigo, symbolizing intuition, insight, and spiritual awareness. This deep, mysterious hue reflects the chakra's qualities of inner vision, visualization, and the exploration of the unseen realms of consciousness. When the Ajna chakra is awakened, we are able to see beyond the limitations of the physical world and perceive the deeper truths that lie beneath the surface of reality, guiding us on our spiritual journey towards self-realization and enlightenment.

However, when the Ajna chakra is blocked or imbalanced, we may experience a range of physical, emotional, and psychological symptoms. These may include feelings of confusion, depression, or disconnection from our inner guidance, as well as an over-reliance on intellectual reasoning and a rejection of spirituality. Physically, imbalances in the Ajna chakra may manifest as headaches, vision problems, or issues with the pituitary gland, reflecting the interconnectedness between our inner state and our physical health.

To balance and activate the Ajna chakra, a variety of yoga exercises and practices can be employed. These may include techniques such as meditating on the Third Eye, Long Chant, Kirtan Kriya, Archer Pose, Whistle Breaths, and Yoga Mudra. Additionally, practicing asanas (poses) where the forehead rests on the floor, such as Child's Pose or

Sphinx Pose, can help to stimulate and energize the Third Eye chakra, facilitating a deeper connection with our intuition and inner wisdom.

In summary, the Ajna chakra serves as the gateway to intuition, wisdom, and spiritual insight, guiding us on our journey towards self-discovery and self-realization. When balanced and activated, it enables us to access higher states of consciousness, gain insights into our true purpose and identity, and navigate life's challenges with clarity and confidence. Through yoga practices and mindful awareness, we can nurture and support the Ajna chakra, awakening to the transformative power of inner vision and aligning with our highest potential as beings of light and wisdom.

SEVENTH CHAKRA: *Sahasrara:* Humility & Vastness
Location: Crown of the head.
Organ/Gland: Brain; pineal gland.
Colour: Violet.
Qualities: The seat of the soul. Connection to the Highest Self. Enlightenment. Unity.
Elevation. Relationship to the Unknown.
Shadow: Grief. The feeling of being separated from existence, and from abundance. Fear of death.
Yoga exercises: Ego Eradicator, Mahabandha, and Sat Kriya. Concentrating on the tip of the nose. All meditation.

The Sahasrara chakra, often referred to as the Crown chakra, stands as the seventh and highest of the primary energy centres within the body according to Hindu and yogic traditions. Positioned at the crown of the head, this chakra symbolizes the pinnacle of spiritual evolution and serves as the gateway to transcendence, humility, and vastness. The Sahasrara chakra is the seat of the soul, representing our connection to the Highest Self, enlightenment, and unity with the divine.

Physiologically, the Sahasrara chakra is closely associated with the brain and the pineal gland, a small endocrine gland located deep within the brain. These structures play crucial roles in regulating our consciousness, perception, and spiritual awareness, as well as in facilitating our connection to higher states of being. When the Sahasrara chakra is balanced and activated, our awareness expands beyond the limitations of the ego, allowing us to experience the vastness of existence and connect with the divine essence within ourselves and all living beings.

The colour associated with the Sahasrara chakra is violet, symbolizing spiritual transformation, wisdom, and enlightenment. This ethereal hue reflects the chakra's qualities of humility, elevation, and reverence for the sacred mysteries of life. When the Sahasrara chakra is awakened, we are able to transcend the illusions of separateness and ego, experiencing a profound sense of unity and interconnectedness with all that is.

However, when the Sahasrara chakra is blocked or imbalanced, we may experience a range of physical, emotional, and psychological symptoms. These may include feelings of grief, isolation, or disconnection from the divine, as well as a fear of death or the unknown. Physically, imbalances in the Sahasrara chakra may manifest as headaches, neurological disorders, or issues with the pineal gland, reflecting the interconnectedness between our inner state and our physical health.

To balance and activate the Sahasrara chakra, various yoga exercises and practices can be employed. These may include techniques such as Ego Eradicator, Mahabandha, Sat Kriya, and concentration on the tip of the nose during meditation. All forms of meditation are particularly potent for opening and aligning the Crown chakra, as they allow us to quiet the mind, transcend the ego, and connect with the divine presence within.

In summary, the Sahasrara chakra serves as the gateway to humility, vastness, and spiritual enlightenment, guiding us on our journey towards unity with the divine. When balanced and activated, it enables us to transcend the limitations of the ego, connect with our Highest Self, and experience the sacredness of existence. Through yoga practices and mindful awareness, we can nurture and support the Sahasrara chakra, awakening to the transformative power of humility and aligning with the infinite wisdom and love of the universe.

EIGHTH CHAKRA: The Aura: Radiance
Location: The electromagnetic field.
Colour: White.
Qualities: The aura combines the effects of all the chakras, and constitutes their total
projection. The aura projects and protects.
Shadow: Shy, withdrawn, vulnerable.
Yoga exercises: Triangle Pose, Ego Eradicator, Archer Pose. All arm exercises. All meditations.

The Eighth Chakra, often referred to as the Aura, stands as an ethereal extension beyond the traditional seven chakras in Hindu and yogic traditions. Unlike the other chakras which have specific physical locations within the body, the Aura encompasses the electromagnetic field surrounding the physical form. It is often depicted as a luminous, radiant energy field that extends beyond the physical body, encompassing and integrating the effects of all the other chakras. The Aura is believed to be a manifestation of our spiritual essence and serves as both a projection and a protective barrier, reflecting the state of our energetic and spiritual well-being.

The colour associated with the Aura is white, symbolizing purity, clarity, and divine radiance. This pristine hue reflects the chakra's qualities of wholeness, completeness, and unity, serving as a conduit for the integration of the energies of all the chakras. When the Aura is balanced and activated, it radiates a luminous glow, reflecting the harmonious alignment of our physical, emotional, and spiritual bodies.

The Aura combines the effects of all the chakras, serving as a holistic projection of our inner state and consciousness. It reflects our thoughts, emotions, and energetic vibrations, as well as the subtle influences of our environment and interactions with others. When the Aura is vibrant and expansive, it acts as a magnet for positive energy, drawing towards us experiences and relationships that are aligned with our highest good. Conversely, when the Aura is clouded or depleted, it may leave us feeling shy, withdrawn, or vulnerable, lacking in confidence and vitality.

To nourish and strengthen the Aura, a variety of yoga exercises and practices can be employed. These may include techniques such as Triangle Pose, Ego Eradicator, Archer Pose, and all arm exercises, which help to stimulate and energize the upper body and promote a sense of strength and resilience. Additionally, all forms of meditation are highly beneficial for enhancing the Aura, as they allow us to cultivate inner peace, clarity, and spiritual connection, radiating these qualities outwards into the world around us.

In summary, the Eighth Chakra, or Aura, serves as the radiant extension of our energetic and spiritual essence, encompassing and integrating the effects of all the other chakras. When balanced and activated, it reflects our inner state of wholeness, completeness, and unity, radiating a luminous glow that attracts positive energy and experiences into our lives. Through yoga practices and mindful awareness, we can nurture and support the Aura, enhancing our energetic field and aligning with the divine radiance that dwells within us.

CHAPTER 6

Music and Stress Relief

WHEN THE SUN fades and all extroversion, entertainment, and distraction is denied to Man, the mind retreats into a state of meditative introversion we call sleep. Thoughts that are unfinished in the mind, during the day, continue throughout the night in the forms of dreams, striving towards their resolution, as part of the brain's intrinsic mechanism to find order. In a sense then, sleep is Nature's way of reuniting Man with him or herself, enabling that which lies dormant in the hidden recesses of the mind, to reveal and express itself in secure isolation from the world.

The dawn of a morning then, has tremendous significance. It is the first witness of the conscious mind to the revelations of the night. To many, the waking hours may express the calm satisfaction of a release, the relief of a burden, and a feeling of pious quietude. To others, however, the meditation of sleep may have brought to the surface of the mind, the most secret burdens of one's life, and leave one in emotional turmoil. Therefore, if one were to provide a general description of the mood of a morning, perhaps it would be one of serenity and depth, holy, while simultaneously tinged with emotions ranging from great disturbance to supreme calmness.

Music has long been revered as a powerful tool for stress relief and emotional well-being, transcending cultural and temporal boundaries to offer solace and comfort to those in need. In contemporary society, where the pressures of daily life can often lead to chronic stress and anxiety, the therapeutic benefits of music have become increasingly recognized and utilized. Research has consistently shown that music can significantly reduce stress levels, enhance mood, and promote relaxation, making it an invaluable resource for mental health and well-being.

One of the primary mechanisms by which music alleviates stress is through its impact on the autonomic nervous system. The autonomic nervous system, which regulates involuntary bodily functions such as heart rate, respiration, and digestion, is divided into the sympathetic and parasympathetic branches. The sympathetic nervous system is responsible for the body's "fight or flight" response, which is activated during times of stress, while the parasympathetic nervous system promotes relaxation and recovery. Listening to soothing music has been shown to activate the parasympathetic nervous system, thereby reducing heart rate, lowering blood pressure, and inducing a state of calm and relaxation.

Moreover, music can influence the release of various neurochemicals that play a role in stress regulation. For instance, music has been found to increase levels of dopamine, a neurotransmitter associated with pleasure and reward, and decrease levels of cortisol, a hormone that is often elevated during periods of stress. The modulation of these neurochemicals not only helps to reduce the physiological symptoms of stress but also enhances emotional well-being, contributing to an overall sense of relaxation and contentment.

The emotional impact of music is another crucial factor in its ability to relieve stress. Music has the power to evoke a wide range of emotions, from joy and excitement to tranquillity and introspection. By engaging with music that resonates with our emotional state, we can experience a sense of catharsis and emotional release, which can be incredibly therapeutic. For example, listening to uplifting and energetic music can boost our mood and provide a much-needed distraction from stressors, while calming and meditative music can help to quiet the mind and foster a sense of inner peace.

Additionally, the rhythm and tempo of music play a significant role in its stress-relieving effects. Slow-tempo music with a steady rhythm has been shown to be particularly effective in promoting relaxation and reducing stress. This type of music can synchronize with our body's natural rhythms, such as heart rate and breathing, creating a state of coherence that enhances relaxation. Conversely, fast-tempo music with a strong beat can energize the body and mind, providing a healthy outlet for releasing pent-up tension and stress.

The therapeutic use of music is not limited to passive listening; active participation in music-making can also be highly beneficial for stress relief. Engaging in activities such as singing, playing an instrument, or dancing can provide a creative outlet for expressing emotions and reducing stress. These activities can also foster a sense of accomplishment and boost self-esteem, further enhancing their therapeutic effects. Group music-making activities, such as choir singing or drumming circles, can also promote social connection and a sense of community, which are important factors in mitigating stress and enhancing well-being.

The use of music therapy as a formal therapeutic intervention has gained widespread recognition in recent years. Music therapy involves the use of music by a trained therapist to address specific physical, emotional, cognitive, and social needs of individuals. It has been shown to be effective in a variety of settings, including hospitals, schools, and mental health facilities, and can benefit individuals of all ages. Music therapy can be tailored to meet the unique needs of each individual, whether it involves listening to music, creating music, or using music as a medium for self-expression and communication.

In medical settings, music therapy has been found to be particularly effective in reducing stress and anxiety in patients undergoing medical procedures or dealing with chronic illnesses. For example, studies have shown that music therapy can significantly reduce preoperative anxiety and postoperative pain in surgical patients, improve mood and quality of life in cancer patients, and enhance coping skills in individuals with chronic pain. The soothing and comforting qualities of music can provide a sense of familiarity and security in stressful and unfamiliar environments, helping patients to feel more relaxed and at ease.

In mental health settings, music therapy can be used to address a wide range of emotional and psychological issues, including depression, anxiety, and post-traumatic stress disorder (PTSD). Music therapy can help individuals to process and express their emotions, develop healthy coping strategies, and build resilience in the face of adversity. For individuals with PTSD, music therapy can provide a safe and non-threatening way to explore and process traumatic memories, helping to reduce symptoms of hyper arousal, avoidance, and negative mood.

The benefits of music for stress relief are not limited to therapeutic settings; incorporating music into daily life can also be an effective way to manage stress and enhance well-being. Creating a personal playlist of favorite songs that evoke positive emotions or promote relaxation can be a simple yet powerful tool for stress relief. Listening to music during daily activities, such as commuting, exercising, or unwinding before bed, can help to create a sense of routine and structure that promotes relaxation and reduces stress.

Furthermore, music can be integrated into mindfulness and meditation practices to enhance their stress-relieving effects. Mindfulness involves paying attention to the present moment with an attitude of openness and acceptance, while meditation involves focusing the mind on a particular object, thought, or activity to achieve a state of mental clarity and calm. Combining music with these practices can deepen the experience of relaxation and mindfulness, helping to quiet the mind and cultivate a sense of inner peace.

In the realm of workplace wellness, music can also play a valuable role in reducing stress and enhancing productivity. Many companies and organizations have started to recognize the benefits of music for employee well-being and have incorporated music-based initiatives into their wellness programs. For example, playing background music in the office can create a more pleasant and relaxed work environment, while offering music therapy sessions or group music-making activities can provide employees with a creative outlet for stress relief and team-building.

Educational institutions have also embraced the benefits of music for stress relief, recognizing its potential to enhance academic performance and support student well-being. Incorporating music into the classroom, whether through music education programs or simply playing background music during study sessions, can help to create a positive and engaging learning environment. Additionally, providing opportunities for students to participate in music-related extracurricular activities, such as choir, band, or orchestra, can promote social connection, self-expression, and emotional resilience.

Music is a powerful and versatile tool for stress relief that transcends cultural and temporal boundaries. Its ability to influence the autonomic nervous system, modulate neurochemical release, evoke emotions, and synchronize with the body's natural rhythms makes it an invaluable resource for promoting relaxation and well-being. Whether through passive listening, active participation, or formal music therapy, music can provide a therapeutic outlet for expressing emotions, reducing stress, and enhancing overall quality of life. By incorporating music into daily routines, therapeutic interventions, and wellness programs, individuals and organizations can harness its transformative power to create a more balanced, harmonious, and stress-free existence.

A musical note has its own distinct psychological effect or emotion, and is also related specifically to a colour, mood, chakra, and time of day.

One of the unique characteristics of Indian music is the assignment of definite times of the day and night for performing or listening Raga melodies. It is believed that only in this period the Raga appears to be at the height of its melodic beauty and majestic splendor. There are some Ragas which are very attractive in the early hours of the mornings; others which appeal in the evenings, yet others which spread their fragrance only near the midnight hour.

This connection of time of the day or night, with the *Raga* or *Ragini* is based on daily cycle of changes that occur in our own body and mind which are constantly undergoing subtle changes. Different moments of the day arouse and stimulate different moods and emotions.

Each *Raga* or *Ragini* is associated with a definite mood or sentiment that nature arouses in human beings. The ancient musicologists were particularly interested in the effects of musical notes, how it affected and enhanced human behavior. Music had the power to cure, to make you feel happy, excited, keep you calm, balance your mind and so on. Extensive research was carried out to find out these effects. This formed the basis of time theory as we know it today.

Emotions, feelings and thoughts have been reported to be greatly influenced by music listening or participation. Emotional experience derived from music has a powerful effect on the formation of one's moral and intellectual outlook. Music activities enhance imagination & creative thinking.

Here is a humble attempt from my part to list the ragas with their therapeutically effects and the appropriate time at which these ragas should be listened. This list will be updated as and when I come across any new raga with their effects and timings. Most of the raga timings given here are taken from various sources.

Managing time stress

Time stress is one of the most common types of stress that we experience today. It is essential to learn how to manage this type of stress if you're going to work productively in a busy organization.

Time stress, a pervasive concern in modern society, arises from the feeling of having too many tasks and not enough time to complete them. This type of stress can have significant implications for both mental and physical health, as well as for personal and professional productivity. Effective time management is crucial for mitigating time stress and involves a combination of strategies, techniques, and mindset shifts designed to optimize the use of one's time, reduce pressure, and enhance overall well-being. By understanding the root causes of time stress and implementing practical solutions, individuals can regain control over their schedules, improve efficiency, and foster a healthier, more balanced lifestyle.

The root causes of time stress often stem from unrealistic expectations, poor planning, procrastination, and a lack of prioritization. Unrealistic expectations can lead to an overwhelming to-do list that is impossible to complete within a given timeframe. This sense of overwhelm can create a vicious cycle of stress, reducing productivity and increasing feelings of inadequacy. To combat this, it is essential to set realistic, achievable goals and break down larger tasks into smaller, manageable steps. This approach not only makes tasks seem less daunting but also provides a sense of accomplishment as each step is completed.

Effective planning is another critical component in managing time stress. Creating a structured schedule that allocates specific time blocks for various tasks can help individuals stay organized and focused. This involves not only planning for work-related activities but also scheduling time for breaks, exercise, and personal activities. Utilizing tools such as calendars, planners, or digital apps can assist in keeping track of deadlines and commitments, ensuring that nothing is overlooked. Additionally, reviewing and adjusting the schedule regularly allows for flexibility and adaptability in response to changing circumstances.

Procrastination is a common contributor to time stress, often driven by fear of failure, perfectionism, or a lack of motivation. Overcoming procrastination requires identifying its underlying causes and developing strategies to address them. Techniques such as the Pomodoro Technique, which involves working in focused intervals followed by short breaks, can enhance concentration and productivity. Setting specific, time-bound goals and rewarding oneself upon completion can also provide motivation to tackle tasks promptly. Moreover, cultivating a growth mind-set, where mistakes are viewed as opportunities for learning rather than failures, can alleviate the fear that often underlies procrastination.

Prioritization is key to effective time management and involves distinguishing between tasks that are urgent, important, or both. The Eisenhower Matrix, a popular prioritization tool, categorizes tasks into four quadrants: urgent and important, important but not urgent, urgent but not important, and neither urgent nor important. This framework helps individuals focus on high-priority tasks that align with their long-term goals while delegating or postponing lower-priority tasks. By concentrating on what truly matters, individuals can make more meaningful progress and reduce the stress associated with juggling multiple responsibilities.

Another aspect of managing time stress is learning to say no. Over commitment is a common issue that stems from a desire to please others or a fear of missing out. However, taking on too many responsibilities can lead to burnout and decreased productivity. Setting boundaries and being selective about commitments allows individuals to focus their energy on tasks that align with their values and priorities. Communicating assertively and respectfully when declining additional responsibilities can help maintain professional and personal relationships while protecting one's time and well-being.

Self-care and stress management practices play a vital role in mitigating time stress. Incorporating regular physical activity, sufficient sleep, healthy eating, and relaxation techniques such as meditation or deep breathing into daily routines can enhance overall well-being and resilience to stress. Exercise, in particular, has been shown to reduce levels of cortisol, the stress hormone, and increase endorphins, which promote a sense of well-being. Ensuring adequate rest and recovery periods prevents burnout and maintains cognitive function and productivity.

Mindfulness and time awareness are also important in managing time stress. Mindfulness involves being fully present in the moment and aware of one's thoughts, feelings, and actions. Practicing mindfulness can help individuals stay focused and reduce the tendency to get distracted or overwhelmed by multiple tasks. Techniques such as mindful breathing, body scans, or mindful walking can be integrated into daily routines to cultivate a state of calm and clarity. Additionally, tracking time spent on various activities can provide insights into patterns and areas where time may be wasted or could be used more efficiently.

Effective delegation and outsourcing are valuable strategies for managing time stress, particularly in professional settings. Delegating tasks to others can free up time for higher-priority activities and ensure that responsibilities are distributed more evenly. This requires clear communication, trust, and the ability to let go of control over certain tasks. Similarly, outsourcing tasks that do not require personal attention, such as administrative work or household chores, can provide additional time for focusing on more important or fulfilling activities.

Technology can be both a source of time stress and a tool for managing it. While constant connectivity and information overload can contribute to stress, leveraging technology effectively can enhance productivity and time management. Tools such as project management software, time tracking apps, and communication platforms can streamline workflows, facilitate collaboration, and keep tasks organized. However, it is crucial to set boundaries with technology use, such as designated periods for checking emails or social media, to prevent it from becoming a distraction.

Work-life balance is a critical consideration in managing time stress. The boundaries between work and personal life have become increasingly blurred, particularly with the rise of remote work. Establishing clear boundaries, such as designated work hours and spaces, can help maintain a balance between professional and personal responsibilities. Taking regular breaks and disconnecting from work-related activities during non-work hours can prevent burnout and ensure time for relaxation and personal pursuits. Employers can support work-life balance by promoting flexible working arrangements and encouraging employees to take time off.

Reflecting on personal values and goals can provide a sense of direction and purpose, helping individuals make more intentional choices about how they spend their time. Aligning daily activities with long-term goals and values can enhance motivation and satisfaction, reducing the stress associated with feeling directionless or unfulfilled. Regularly reassessing priorities and making adjustments as needed ensures that time is spent on what truly matters, fostering a sense of accomplishment and well-being.

In addition to individual strategies, organizational culture and policies play a significant role in managing time stress. Employers can create a supportive environment by promoting a healthy work-life balance, providing resources for time management training, and fostering a culture of open communication and realistic expectations. Encouraging regular feedback and collaboration can help identify and address sources of time stress, leading to a more productive and satisfied workforce.

In educational settings, teaching time management skills to students can equip them with tools to handle academic pressures and future professional responsibilities. Incorporating time management training into curricula, providing resources such as planners and digital tools, and encouraging a balanced approach to academic and extracurricular activities can help students develop effective habits early on.

Family and community support are also important in managing time stress. Sharing responsibilities within the household, seeking support from family and friends, and participating in community activities can provide a sense of connection and reduce the burden of time stress. Building a network of support allows for the sharing of tasks and emotional support, fostering resilience and well-being.

Managing time stress requires a multifaceted approach that combines effective planning, prioritization, self-care, and support systems. By setting realistic goals, breaking tasks into manageable steps, and utilizing tools and techniques for organization and focus, individuals can optimize their use of time and reduce stress. Overcoming procrastination, learning to say no, and delegating tasks can free up valuable time for high-priority activities and self-care. Incorporating mindfulness and stress management practices into daily routines enhances resilience and well-being, while technology and organizational support can further streamline workflows and promote a healthy work-life balance. Reflecting on personal values and goals ensures that time is spent on meaningful activities, fostering a sense of purpose and satisfaction. Through these strategies, individuals can regain control over their schedules, improve efficiency, and lead a healthier, more balanced life.

First, learn good time management skills. This can include using To-Do Lists or, if you have to manage many simultaneous projects, Action Programs etc.

Next, make sure that you're devoting enough time to your important priorities. Unfortunately, it's easy to get caught up in seemingly urgent tasks which actually have little impact on your overall objectives. This can leave you feeling exhausted, or feeling that you worked a full day yet accomplished nothing meaningful.

Your important tasks are usually the ones that will help you reach your goals, and working on these projects is a better use of your time. Our article on prioritization helps you separate tasks that you need to focus on from those you can safely put off.

If you often feel that you don't have enough time to complete all of your tasks, learn how to create more time in your day. This might mean coming in early or working late, so that you have quiet time to focus. You should also use your peak working time to concentrate on your most important tasks – because you're working more efficiently, this helps you do more with the time you have.

For instance, if you're a morning person, schedule the tasks that need the greatest concentration during this time. Our article "Is This a Morning Task" helps you learn how to prioritize your tasks and schedule them during your most productive times of day. You can leave less important tasks, like checking email, for times when your energy levels drop.

Also, make sure that you're polite but assertive about saying "no" to tasks that you don't have the capacity to do.

Managing Anticipatory Stress

Anticipatory stress refers to the anxiety and tension experienced in anticipation of a future event or situation that is perceived as threatening or challenging. Unlike immediate stress, which occurs in response to a current stressor, anticipatory stress is rooted in the anticipation of what might happen. This type of stress can be pervasive and debilitating, as it often involves ruminating on worst-case scenarios, which can lead to chronic anxiety, impaired decision-making, and reduced quality of life. Effective management of anticipatory stress requires a multifaceted approach that addresses both the cognitive and emotional aspects of this form of anxiety.

The root cause of anticipatory stress often lies in cognitive distortions and an overactive imagination. People who experience high levels of anticipatory stress tend to engage in catastrophic thinking, imagining worst-case scenarios that may never come to pass. This negative thinking pattern can create a self-fulfilling prophecy, where the fear of a negative outcome increases the likelihood of stress and reduces one's ability to cope effectively. Cognitive-behavioural techniques can be particularly useful in addressing these distortions. By identifying and challenging irrational thoughts, individuals can reframe their thinking and reduce the impact of anticipatory stress.

Mindfulness and meditation are powerful tools for managing anticipatory stress. Mindfulness involves focusing on the present moment and accepting it without judgment. This practice can help individuals break the cycle of ruminative thinking that fuels anticipatory stress. Meditation techniques such as deep breathing, progressive muscle relaxation, and guided imagery can promote relaxation and help individuals stay grounded in the present. Regular practice of these techniques can build resilience against stress and improve overall mental well-being.

Time management and organization can also play a critical role in reducing anticipatory stress. Often, stress about future events is exacerbated by a lack of preparation or a feeling of being overwhelmed by tasks. Breaking tasks into smaller, manageable steps and creating a structured plan can provide a sense of control and reduce anxiety. Using tools such as planners, to-do lists, and digital apps can help individuals keep track of their responsibilities and deadlines, ensuring that they are well-prepared for upcoming events.

Another effective strategy for managing anticipatory stress is developing problem-solving skills. When faced with a potential future challenge, individuals can benefit from a proactive approach that involves identifying possible solutions and developing a plan of action. This can transform feelings of helplessness into a sense of empowerment and readiness. Techniques such as brainstorming, evaluating the pros and cons of different options, and seeking advice from others can enhance problem-solving abilities and reduce stress.

Physical activity is a well-documented stress reliever that can help manage anticipatory stress. Regular exercise has been shown to reduce levels of stress hormones such as cortisol and increase the production of endorphins, which are natural mood elevators. Engaging in physical activities such as walking, running, yoga, or sports can provide a healthy outlet for releasing tension and improving mood. Additionally, exercise can serve as a distraction from ruminative thoughts and provide a sense of accomplishment and control.

Social support is another crucial factor in managing anticipatory stress. Sharing concerns with trusted friends, family members, or a support group can provide emotional relief and offer different perspectives on the situation. Social connections can also provide practical support and encouragement, helping individuals feel less isolated and more capable of handling future challenges. Building and maintaining a strong support network is essential for resilience and well-being.

Professional help can be invaluable for individuals struggling with severe anticipatory stress. Therapists and counsellors can offer techniques and strategies tailored to an individual's specific needs. Cognitive-behavioural therapy (CBT), for instance, is particularly effective in addressing the thought patterns that contribute to anticipatory stress. Therapy can provide a safe space to explore fears, develop coping mechanisms, and build resilience. In some cases, medication may be prescribed to manage symptoms of anxiety, allowing individuals to engage more fully in therapeutic work.

Building resilience through positive lifestyle changes can also help manage anticipatory stress. Adopting healthy habits such as a balanced diet, adequate sleep, and regular relaxation practices can improve overall well-being and make it easier to cope with stress. Avoiding excessive caffeine and alcohol, which can exacerbate anxiety, is also important. Establishing a routine that includes time for hobbies, social activities, and self-care can provide balance and prevent stress from becoming overwhelming.

Acceptance and commitment therapy (ACT) is another approach that can be effective in managing anticipatory stress. ACT encourages individuals to accept their thoughts and feelings rather than trying to eliminate them, while committing to actions that align with their values. This approach can help individuals develop a more flexible and adaptive response to stress, reducing the impact of anticipatory anxiety on their lives. Techniques such as mindfulness, values clarification, and cognitive diffusion are central to ACT and can be integrated into daily practice.

Developing emotional intelligence can also be beneficial in managing anticipatory stress. Emotional intelligence involves the ability to recognize, understand, and manage one's own emotions, as well as the emotions of others. Enhancing emotional intelligence can improve self-awareness, self-regulation, and empathy, which are important skills for coping with stress. Training in emotional intelligence can include activities such as reflective journaling, practicing active listening, and seeking feedback from others.

Creative outlets can provide a powerful means of managing anticipatory stress. Engaging in creative activities such as art, music, writing, or dance can offer a therapeutic release for emotions and provide a distraction from stress. Creative expression can also help individuals process and make sense of their fears and anxieties, leading to greater insight and emotional relief. Incorporating creative activities into daily or weekly routines can enhance overall well-being and provide a valuable tool for stress management.

Spiritual practices and beliefs can also play a significant role in managing anticipatory stress. For many individuals, spiritual practices such as prayer, meditation, or participation in religious or spiritual communities provide comfort, support, and a sense of meaning and purpose. These practices can offer a framework for understanding and coping with stress, fostering resilience and inner peace. Exploring and integrating spiritual practices that resonate with one's beliefs and values can be a powerful source of strength and comfort.

Exposure therapy is another technique that can be useful for managing anticipatory stress, particularly when it involves specific fears or phobias. Exposure therapy involves gradually and systematically exposing oneself to the feared situation or object in a controlled and safe manner. This process can help desensitize individuals to the stressor and reduce the anxiety associated with anticipation. Working with a trained therapist, individuals can develop a plan for exposure that includes relaxation techniques and coping strategies to manage anxiety.

Incorporating humour and play into daily life can also help manage anticipatory stress. Laughter and playfulness can reduce stress hormones, increase endorphins, and improve overall mood. Engaging in activities that bring joy and laughter, such as watching a comedy, playing games, or spending time with playful friends or pets, can provide a refreshing break from stress and enhance emotional well-being. Cultivating a sense of humour and allowing oneself to experience joy and play can be an effective way to counterbalance the effects of anticipatory stress.

Incorporating relaxation techniques such as deep breathing, progressive muscle relaxation, and guided imagery can help manage anticipatory stress by promoting physical and mental relaxation. Deep breathing exercises involve taking slow, deep breaths to calm the nervous system and reduce anxiety. Progressive muscle relaxation involves tensing and then relaxing different muscle groups to release tension. Guided imagery involves visualizing peaceful and calming scenes to reduce stress. These techniques can be practiced regularly to build relaxation skills and reduce the impact of anticipatory stress.

Building resilience through positive self-talk and affirmations can also help manage anticipatory stress. Positive self-talk involves challenging negative thoughts and replacing them with more constructive and empowering ones. Affirmations are positive statements that reinforce self-belief and confidence. Practicing positive self-talk and using affirmations can help individuals develop a more optimistic and resilient mind-set, reducing the impact of anticipatory stress. Regularly repeating affirmations and consciously shifting negative thoughts can build mental strength and resilience.

In summary, managing anticipatory stress requires a comprehensive approach that addresses cognitive, emotional, and behavioural aspects of stress. Techniques such as cognitive-behavioural therapy, mindfulness, meditation, time management, and problem-solving can help individuals reduce anxiety and gain control over their thoughts and actions. Physical activity, social support, professional help, and positive lifestyle changes can enhance resilience and well-being. Acceptance and commitment therapy, emotional intelligence, creative outlets, spiritual practices, exposure therapy, humour, relaxation techniques, and positive self-talk are all valuable tools for managing anticipatory stress. By integrating these strategies into daily life, individuals can reduce the impact of anticipatory stress, improve mental and physical health, and achieve a more balanced and fulfilling life.

Because anticipatory stress is future based, start by recognizing that the event you're dreading doesn't have to play out as you imagine. Use positive visualization techniques to imagine the situation going right.

Research shows that your mind often can't tell the difference, on a basic neurological level, between a situation that you've visualized going well repeatedly and one that's actually happened.

Other techniques – like meditation – will help you develop focus and the ability to concentrate on what's happening right now, rather than on an imagined future. Consider setting aside time daily – even if it's only five minutes – to meditate.

Anticipatory stress can result from a lack of confidence. For example, you might be stressing over a presentation that you are giving next week, because you are afraid that your presentation won't be interesting. Often, addressing these personal fears directly will lower your stress. In this example, if you put in extra time to practice and prepare for tough questions, you'll likely feel more prepared for the event.

Last, learn how to overcome a fear of failure: by making contingency plans and analysing all of the possible outcomes, you'll get a clearer idea of what could happen in the future. This can help diminish your fear of failure and give you a greater sense of control over events.

Managing Situational Stress

Situational stress often appears suddenly, for example, you might get caught in a situation that you completely failed to anticipate. To manage situational stress better, learn to be more self-aware. This means recognizing the "automatic" physical and emotional signals that your body sends out when you are under pressure.

For example, imagine that the meeting you are in suddenly dissolves into a shouting match between team members. Your automatic response is to feel a surge of anxiety. Your stomach knots and feels bloated. You withdraw into yourself and, if someone asks for your input, you have a difficult time knowing what to say.

Situational stress arises from specific circumstances or events that disrupt an individual's sense of stability and well-being. This type of stress is typically acute, triggered by immediate pressures or challenges such as a demanding work deadline, a major life change, a conflict, or an unexpected crisis. While situational stress can be intense, it is usually temporary and can be managed effectively with appropriate strategies and coping mechanisms. Understanding the nature of situational stress and implementing comprehensive management techniques can help individuals navigate these challenges with resilience and maintain their overall health and well-being.

The first step in managing situational stress is to identify the source of stress and understand its impact. Recognizing what specific event or situation is causing stress can help in developing a targeted approach to address it. This involves paying attention to physical, emotional, and cognitive signs of stress, such as tension, irritability, anxiety, and difficulty concentrating. Keeping a stress journal can be a useful tool for tracking stressors and reactions, providing insights into patterns and triggers that can inform stress management strategies.

Once the source of stress is identified, problem-solving techniques can be employed to address the immediate issue. Problem-solving involves breaking down the stressful situation into manageable components, identifying possible solutions, and evaluating the pros and cons of each option. Developing a clear plan of action can provide a sense of control and direction, reducing feelings of helplessness and anxiety. It is important to be flexible and willing to adjust the plan as needed, as situations may evolve and require new approaches.

Time management is a critical aspect of handling situational stress, particularly when it involves deadlines or multiple responsibilities. Effective time management strategies include prioritizing tasks, setting realistic goals, and creating a structured schedule. Tools such as calendars, planners, and digital apps can assist in organizing tasks and tracking progress. Allocating specific time blocks for different activities, including breaks and relaxation, ensures a balanced approach to managing responsibilities and prevents burnout.

Incorporating relaxation techniques into daily routines can significantly reduce situational stress. Techniques such as deep breathing, progressive muscle relaxation, and mindfulness meditation can help calm the mind and body, reducing the physiological effects of stress. Deep breathing exercises, for instance, involve taking slow, deep breaths to activate the body's relaxation response, lowering heart rate and blood pressure. Progressive muscle relaxation involves tensing and then relaxing different muscle groups, releasing physical tension and promoting a sense of calm. Mindfulness meditation encourages focusing on the present moment without judgment, helping to break the cycle of stress-inducing thoughts.

Physical activity is another effective way to manage situational stress. Regular exercise has been shown to reduce stress hormones such as cortisol and increase endorphins, which enhance mood and provide a sense of well-being. Activities such as walking, running, yoga, or dancing can serve as healthy outlets for releasing tension and improving overall fitness. Even short bursts of physical activity throughout the day can make a significant difference in managing stress and boosting energy levels.

Social support plays a crucial role in mitigating situational stress. Talking to friends, family members, or colleagues about stressful situations can provide emotional relief and offer different perspectives and advice. Sharing experiences and feelings with trusted individuals can reduce feelings of isolation and provide a sense of connection and support. In addition to personal networks, professional support from counsellors, therapists, or support groups can offer specialized guidance and coping strategies tailored to individual needs.

Effective communication is essential in managing situational stress, particularly in interpersonal conflicts or work-related pressures. Developing assertive communication skills can help individuals express their needs, set boundaries, and resolve conflicts constructively. This involves being clear, direct, and respectful in interactions, actively listening to others, and finding mutually beneficial solutions. Improved communication can reduce misunderstandings and tensions, fostering healthier relationships and a more supportive environment.

Another key strategy for managing situational stress is maintaining a healthy lifestyle. This includes a balanced diet, adequate sleep, and avoiding excessive use of substances such as caffeine, alcohol, or drugs that can exacerbate stress. Eating a nutritious diet with plenty of fruits, vegetables, lean proteins, and whole grains provides the energy and nutrients needed to cope with stress. Ensuring sufficient sleep is crucial for physical and mental recovery, as sleep deprivation can increase stress and impair cognitive function. Establishing a regular sleep routine and creating a restful sleep environment can enhance sleep quality and overall resilience to stress.

Cognitive-behavioural techniques can be particularly effective in managing situational stress by addressing the thoughts and beliefs that contribute to stress reactions. Cognitive restructuring involves identifying and challenging irrational or negative thoughts and replacing them with more balanced and constructive ones. This can help reduce the intensity of stress responses and promote a more positive outlook. Practicing gratitude, focusing on positive aspects of life, and using affirmations can also shift attention away from stressors and foster a sense of appreciation and optimism.

In some cases, situational stress may require specific coping strategies tailored to the nature of the stressor. For instance, preparing for a major presentation or exam might involve focused study sessions, practice runs, and relaxation techniques to manage performance anxiety. Dealing with a significant life change, such as moving to a new city or starting a new job, might involve creating a support network, researching the new environment, and allowing time for adjustment. Tailoring coping strategies to the specific context of the stressor can enhance their effectiveness and provide targeted relief.

Humour and play can also be valuable tools in managing situational stress. Laughter has been shown to reduce stress hormones, increase endorphins, and improve overall mood. Engaging in activities that bring joy and laughter, such as watching a comedy, playing games, or spending time with playful friends or pets, can provide a refreshing break from stress and enhance emotional well-being. Cultivating a sense of humour and allowing oneself to experience joy and play can be an effective way to counterbalance the effects of stress.

Developing resilience is another important aspect of managing situational stress. Resilience involves the ability to bounce back from adversity and maintain a positive outlook despite challenges. Building resilience can involve developing a growth mind-set, where difficulties are viewed as opportunities for learning and growth. Setting realistic goals, maintaining a sense of purpose, and fostering strong social connections can also enhance resilience. Engaging in regular self-reflection and self-care practices can support ongoing personal development and emotional strength.

In addition to individual strategies, organizational and community support can play a significant role in managing situational stress. Employers can create supportive work environments by promoting work-life balance, providing resources for stress management, and encouraging open communication and collaboration. Schools and community organizations can offer programs and services that address stress and provide support for individuals facing specific challenges. Creating a culture of support and understanding within organizations and communities can enhance collective resilience and well-being.

Professional help can be invaluable for individuals struggling with severe situational stress. Therapists and counsellors can offer techniques and strategies tailored to an individual's specific needs. Cognitive-behavioural therapy (CBT), for instance, is particularly effective in addressing the thought patterns that contribute to stress. Therapy can provide a safe space to explore fears, develop coping mechanisms, and build resilience. In some cases, medication may be prescribed to manage symptoms of anxiety, allowing individuals to engage more fully in therapeutic work.

Reflecting on personal values and goals can provide a sense of direction and purpose, helping individuals make more intentional choices about how they respond to situational stress. Aligning actions with long-term goals and values can enhance motivation and satisfaction, reducing the stress associated with feeling directionless or unfulfilled.

Regularly reassessing priorities and making adjustments as needed ensures that efforts are focused on what truly matters, fostering a sense of accomplishment and well-being.

Building emotional intelligence can also be beneficial in managing situational stress. Emotional intelligence involves the ability to recognize, understand, and manage one's own emotions, as well as the emotions of others. Enhancing emotional intelligence can improve self-awareness, self-regulation, and empathy, which are important skills for coping with stress. Training in emotional intelligence can include activities such as reflective journaling, practicing active listening, and seeking feedback from others.

Incorporating spiritual practices and beliefs can also play a significant role in managing situational stress. For many individuals, spiritual practices such as prayer, meditation, or participation in religious or spiritual communities provide comfort, support, and a sense of meaning and purpose. These practices can offer a framework for understanding and coping with stress, fostering resilience and inner peace. Exploring and integrating spiritual practices that resonate with one's beliefs and values can be a powerful source of strength and comfort.

Managing situational stress requires a comprehensive approach that addresses cognitive, emotional, and behavioural aspects of stress. Techniques such as problem-solving, time management, relaxation, physical activity, social support, effective communication, and maintaining a healthy lifestyle can help individuals reduce anxiety and gain control over their reactions to stress. Cognitive-behavioural techniques, humour, play, resilience-building, and professional help can further enhance coping abilities. Reflecting on personal values, developing emotional intelligence, and incorporating spiritual practices can provide additional support and strength. By integrating these strategies into daily life, individuals can navigate situational stress with resilience, improve their mental and physical health, and achieve a more balanced and fulfilling life.

Conflict is a major source of situational stress. Learn effective conflict resolution skills, so that you are well-prepared to handle the stress of conflict when it arises. It's also important to learn how to manage conflict in meetings, since resolving group conflict can be different from resolving individual issues.

Everyone reacts to situational stress differently, and it is essential that you understand both the physical and emotional symptoms of this stress, so that you can manage them appropriately. For instance, if your natural tendency is to withdraw emotionally, then learn how to think on your feet and communicate better during these situations. If your natural response is to get angry and shout, then learn how to manage your emotions.

Managing Encounter Stress

Encounter stress, a specific form of stress that arises from direct interactions with people, can be particularly challenging because it involves immediate, face-to-face encounters that often trigger intense emotional responses. Managing this type of stress effectively requires a multifaceted approach that includes enhancing emotional intelligence, improving communication skills, developing conflict resolution strategies, and incorporating various coping mechanisms. This comprehensive strategy helps individuals navigate interpersonal interactions more smoothly, maintain emotional balance, and foster healthier relationships.

One of the foundational steps in managing encounter stress is developing emotional intelligence. Emotional intelligence involves the ability to recognize, understand, and manage one's own emotions, as well as the emotions of others. By enhancing emotional intelligence, individuals can better identify their emotional triggers and understand how these affect their interactions. Techniques to build emotional intelligence include reflective journaling, mindfulness practices, and seeking feedback from others about one's emotional responses and interactions. Self-awareness, a key component of emotional intelligence, allows individuals to pause and consider their emotional state before reacting, thereby reducing impulsive reactions that can exacerbate stress.

Effective communication is crucial in managing encounter stress, as communication breakdowns often amplify stress in interpersonal interactions. Clear, assertive communication helps prevent misunderstandings and reduce tensions. Assertive communication involves expressing one's needs, thoughts, and feelings directly and respectfully, without aggression or passivity. For instance, using "I" statements, such as "I feel overwhelmed when deadlines are changed at the last minute," helps convey feelings without blaming or criticizing others. Active listening, another vital communication skill, involves fully concentrating, understanding, responding, and remembering what the other person is saying. This not only aids in understanding the other person's perspective but also demonstrates respect and fosters a cooperative atmosphere.

Conflict resolution skills are integral to managing encounter stress, especially in situations involving interpersonal conflicts. Effective conflict resolution requires addressing the underlying issues rather than merely the surface symptoms. Techniques such as seeking common ground, focusing on interests rather than positions, and brainstorming solutions that satisfy both parties can lead to more constructive outcomes. Approaching conflicts with a problem-solving mind-set, seeing them as opportunities for growth and understanding, rather than threats, can significantly reduce stress. Training in conflict resolution, through workshops or mediation programs, can provide valuable skills and strategies to handle conflicts more effectively.

Stress management techniques such as deep breathing, progressive muscle relaxation, and mindfulness meditation can be highly effective in reducing the physiological symptoms of stress that often accompany stressful encounters. Deep breathing exercises can help calm the nervous system and reduce immediate stress responses. Progressive muscle relaxation, which involves tensing and then relaxing different muscle groups, can help release physical tension associated with stress. Mindfulness meditation encourages focusing on the present moment without judgment, helping individuals stay grounded and reduce the impact of stress-inducing thoughts and emotions. Regular practice of these techniques can build resilience against stress and improve overall mental well-being.

Building and maintaining healthy relationships can significantly reduce encounter stress. Positive social interactions provide emotional support, foster a sense of belonging, and enhance overall well-being. Investing time and effort in developing strong, supportive relationships can create a buffer against stress. This involves being open, honest, and empathetic in interactions and actively working to resolve conflicts and misunderstandings. Social support networks, including friends, family, and colleagues, can offer practical assistance and emotional comfort during stressful times. Engaging in social activities, such as group sports, clubs, or community events, can provide opportunities for positive interactions and stress relief.

Setting boundaries is another essential strategy for managing encounter stress. Clear boundaries help protect one's emotional and physical well-being and prevent burnout. This involves understanding one's limits and communicating them effectively to others. For example, setting limits on work hours, saying no to additional responsibilities when overwhelmed, or taking time for oneself when needed. Boundaries can also involve limiting interactions with individuals who are consistently stressful or draining. Learning to assertively set and maintain boundaries is crucial for protecting one's well-being and reducing encounter stress.

Self-care practices are vital in managing encounter stress. Self-care involves engaging in activities that promote physical, emotional, and mental health. This can include regular exercise, healthy eating, sufficient sleep, hobbies, and relaxation activities. Self-care helps replenish energy and resilience, making it easier to handle stressful encounters. Incorporating self-care into daily routines ensures that one's well-being is prioritized, which can significantly reduce the impact of stress. Activities such as reading, listening to music, spending time in nature, or practicing yoga can provide restorative benefits and enhance overall well-being.

Developing resilience is crucial in managing encounter stress. Resilience involves the ability to bounce back from adversity and maintain a positive outlook despite challenges. Building resilience can involve developing a growth mind-set, where difficulties are viewed as opportunities for learning and growth. Setting realistic goals, maintaining a sense of purpose, and fostering strong social connections can also enhance resilience. Engaging in regular self-reflection and self-care practices can support ongoing personal development and emotional strength.

Professional help can be invaluable for individuals struggling with severe encounter stress. Therapists and counsellors can offer techniques and strategies tailored to an individual's specific needs. Cognitive-behavioural therapy (CBT), for instance, is particularly effective in addressing the thought patterns that contribute to stress. Therapy can provide a safe space to explore fears, develop coping mechanisms, and build resilience. In some cases, medication may be prescribed to manage symptoms of anxiety, allowing individuals to engage more fully in therapeutic work.

Incorporating humour and play into daily life can also help manage encounter stress. Laughter and playfulness can reduce stress hormones, increase endorphins, and improve overall mood. Engaging in activities that bring joy and laughter, such as watching a comedy, playing games, or spending time with playful friends or pets, can provide a refreshing break from stress and enhance emotional well-being. Cultivating a sense of humour and allowing oneself to experience joy and play can be an effective way to counterbalance the effects of stress.

Exploring and integrating spiritual practices can also play a significant role in managing encounter stress. For many individuals, spiritual practices such as prayer, meditation, or participation in religious or spiritual communities provide comfort, support, and a sense of meaning and purpose. These practices can offer a framework for understanding and coping with stress, fostering resilience and inner peace. Exploring and integrating spiritual practices that resonate with one's beliefs and values can be a powerful source of strength and comfort.

Mindfulness practices are particularly effective in managing encounter stress. Mindfulness involves being fully present in the moment and observing thoughts and feelings without judgment. This practice can help individuals remain calm and centered during stressful encounters, reducing the likelihood of being overwhelmed by emotions. Techniques such as mindfulness meditation, mindful breathing, and mindful walking can help cultivate a state of calm and awareness. Regular mindfulness practice can enhance overall emotional regulation and resilience, making it easier to handle stress in daily interactions.

Developing a support system within professional environments can also help manage encounter stress, especially in the workplace where interactions with colleagues and supervisors are a common source of stress. Creating a positive work culture that encourages open communication, teamwork, and mutual respect can reduce stress levels. Employers can provide resources such as employee assistance programs, stress management workshops, and access to counselling services. Encouraging a healthy work-life balance, recognizing achievements, and fostering a supportive work environment can enhance job satisfaction and reduce encounter stress.

Learning to manage expectations is another important aspect of handling encounter stress. Unrealistic expectations about oneself and others can lead to disappointment and frustration. It is important to set realistic, achievable goals and to be flexible and adaptable in the face of changing circumstances. Practicing self-compassion and recognizing that it is okay to make mistakes and experience setbacks can reduce self-imposed pressure. Being patient with oneself and others and adjusting expectations can help alleviate stress and promote a more positive outlook.

Developing coping mechanisms for handling difficult personalities can also be beneficial in managing encounter stress. Difficult personalities, whether in personal or professional settings, can be a significant source of stress. Strategies such as setting clear boundaries, staying calm, and not taking negative behaviour personally can help manage interactions with challenging individuals. Learning to assertively address problematic behaviour and seeking support from others when needed can also be effective. Understanding that one cannot change another person's behaviour but can control one's own responses can empower individuals to handle difficult interactions with greater ease.

In summary, managing encounter stress requires a comprehensive approach that addresses emotional, cognitive, and behavioural aspects of stress. Enhancing emotional intelligence, improving communication skills, and developing conflict resolution strategies are foundational steps in reducing stress in interpersonal interactions. Incorporating stress management techniques, building healthy relationships, and setting boundaries can further support stress reduction. Self-care practices, resilience building, and professional help provide additional layers of support. Incorporating humour, play, and spiritual practices can offer emotional relief and strength. Mindfulness practices, support systems within professional environments, managing expectations, and developing coping mechanisms for difficult personalities round out a holistic approach to managing encounter stress. By integrating these strategies into daily life, individuals can navigate stressful encounters with greater resilience, improve their mental and physical health, and foster more positive and fulfilling relationships.

Because encounter stress is focused entirely on people, you'll manage this type of stress better by working on your people skills. To find out how good your people skills are, take our quiz, and discover the areas that you need to develop.

A good place to start is to develop greater emotional intelligence. Emotional intelligence is the ability to recognize the emotions, wants, and needs of yourself and of others. This is an important skill in interacting with others and in building good relationships.

It's also important to know when you're about to reach your limit for interactions in the day. Everyone has different symptoms for encounter stress, but a common one is withdrawing psychologically from others and working mechanically. Another common symptom is getting cranky, cold, or impersonal with others in your interactions. When you start to experience these symptoms, do whatever you can to take a break. Go for a walk, drink water, and practice deep breathing exercises.

Empathy is a valuable skill for coping with this type of stress, because it allows you to see the situation from the other person's perspective. This gives you greater understanding and helps you to structure your communications so that you address the other person's feelings, wants, and needs.

35 EMOTIONS AND THEIR CLASSIFICATIONS

Negative and Forceful	Anger
	Annoyance
	Contempt
	Disgust
	Irritation
Negative and not in Control	Anxiety
	Embarrassment
	Fear
	Helplessness
	Powerlessness
	Worry
Negative Thoughts	Doubt
	Envy
	Frustration
	Guilt
	Shame
Negative and Passive	Boredom
	Despair
	Disappointment
	Hurt
	Sadness
Agitation	Stress
	Shock
	Tension
Positive and Lively	Amusement
	Delight
	Elation
	Excitement
	Happiness
	Joy
	Pleasure
Caring	Affection
	Empathy
	Friendly
	Love

ANOTHER CLASSIFICATION OF EMOTIONS

Primary Emotion	Secondary Emotion	Tertiary Emotion
Love	Affection	Adoration Fondness Liking Attractiveness Caring Tenderness Compassion Sentimentality
	Lust/ Sexual Desire	Desire Passion Infatuation
	Longing	Longing
Joy	Cheerfulness	Amusement Bliss Gaiety Glee Jolliness Joviality Joy Delight Enjoyment Gladness Happiness Jubilation Elation Satisfaction Ecstasy Euphoria
	Zest	Enthusiasm Zeal Excitement Thrill Exhilaration
	Contentment	Pleasure
	Pride	Triumph
	Optimism	Eagerness Hope
	Enthrallment	Enthrallment Rapture
	Relief	Relief

Surprise	Surprise	Amazement Astonishment
Anger	Irritability Exasperation Rage Disgust Envy Torment	

Plutchik's wheel of emotions

Robert Plutchik (21 October 1927 – 29 April 2006) was professor at the Albert Einstein College of Medicine and adjunct professor at the University of South Florida. His research interests include the study of emotions, the study of suicide and violence, and the study of the psychotherapy process. His psycho-evolutionary theory of emotion is one of the most influential classification approaches for general emotional responses. He considered there to be eight primary emotions—anger, fear, sadness, disgust, surprise, anticipation, trust, and joy. Plutchik argues for the primacy of these emotions by showing each to be the trigger of behaviour with high survival value.

Basic emotion	Basic opposite
Joy	*Sadness*
Trust	*Disgust*
Fear	*Anger*
Surprise	*Anticipation*

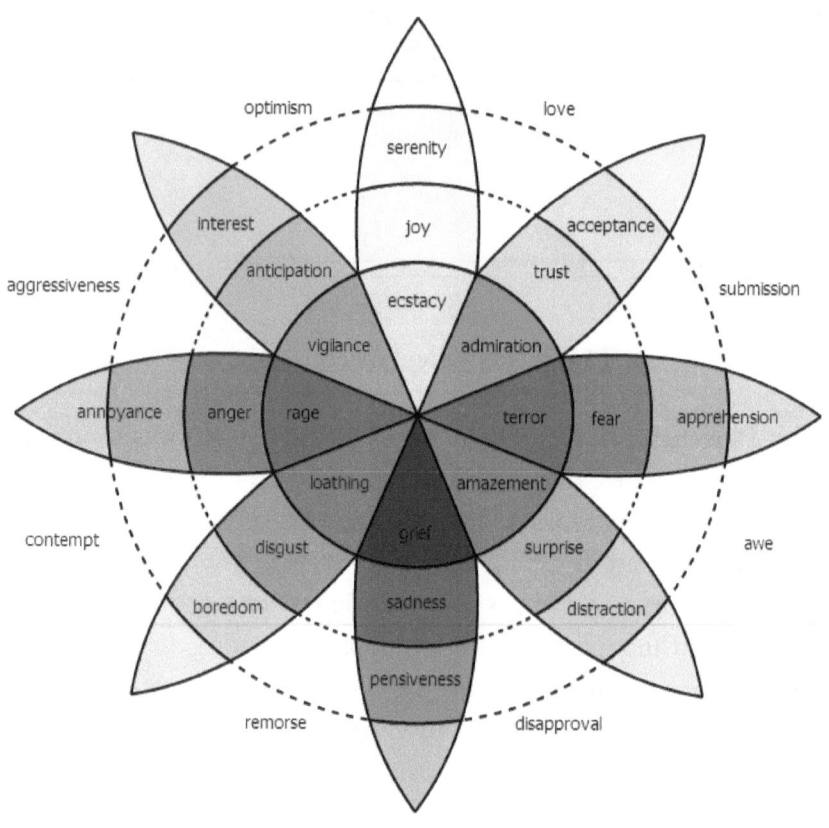

RAGAS AND THEIR TIMINGS

Indian classical music, with its rich tradition and complexity, places significant emphasis on the timing of ragas, which are melodic frameworks for improvisation and composition. The time theory of ragas, which prescribes specific times of the day or night for performing particular ragas, is integral to the practice and appreciation of this musical form. This system is based on the belief that the time of day influences the emotional impact and spiritual efficacy of the raga. This alignment of ragas with the natural rhythms of the day enhances the aesthetic and emotional experience for both the performer and the listener. Understanding the connection between ragas and their timings involves delving into the historical, theoretical, and practical aspects of this unique musical tradition.

The concept of time theory in Indian classical music is deeply rooted in ancient texts and traditions. The earliest references to the time-specific performance of ragas can be found in ancient Indian scriptures such as the "Natyashastra" by Bharata Muni and the "Sangita Ratnakara" by Sarangadeva. These texts lay the foundation for associating ragas with specific times of the day, a practice that has been meticulously followed and refined over centuries. The rationale behind this practice is that different times of the day evoke different moods and emotions, and certain ragas are believed to resonate more profoundly with these natural moods.

Indian classical music, encompassing both Hindustani (North Indian) and Carnatic (South Indian) traditions, has distinct time slots for performing ragas. In the Hindustani tradition, the day is divided into eight time segments, each approximately three hours long, starting from dawn and ending at midnight. Each segment is associated with specific ragas that are believed to be most effective and appropriate during that time. This division aligns with the circadian rhythms and the changes in nature and human physiology throughout the day.

The early morning hours, from 4 AM to 7 AM, are considered ideal for performing ragas like Bhairav, Todi, and Lalit. These ragas, often composed in serious and contemplative moods, evoke a sense of tranquillity and introspection. The serene atmosphere of the pre-dawn hours, when the world is still and quiet, enhances the meditative quality of these ragas. Bhairav, with its solemn and majestic tone, is particularly effective in creating a devotional and introspective mood, making it a perfect start to the day.

As the day progresses, the late morning hours from 7 AM to 10 AM are suited for ragas such as Bilawal, Deshkar, and Jaunpuri. These ragas, typically more lively and uplifting, reflect the increasing activity and energy of the morning. Bilawal, a raga characterized by its pure and joyful notes, resonates with the freshness and vitality of the morning, creating a sense of optimism and enthusiasm.

The mid-morning to noon hours, from 10 AM to 1 PM, are associated with ragas like Sarang, Bhimpalasi, and Gaud Sarang. These ragas, with their bright and vibrant tones, match the peak of daytime activity and the full light of the sun. Sarang, known for its cheerful and spirited nature, embodies the energy and dynamism of the midday, making it a popular choice for performances during this time.

The afternoon hours, from 1 PM to 4 PM, are reserved for ragas such as Multani, Patdeep, and Madhuvanti. These ragas often have a gentle and soothing quality, providing a sense of relaxation and calm as the day transitions from the hectic morning to the more relaxed afternoon. Multani, with its poignant and expressive notes, evokes a sense of longing and introspection, complementing the languid atmosphere of the afternoon.

The late afternoon to early evening period, from 4 PM to 7 PM, is ideal for ragas like Yaman, Shuddh Kalyan, and Hameer. These ragas, with their serene and graceful melodies, mirror the fading light of the day and the onset of dusk. Yaman, one of the most popular evening ragas, is known for its soothing and melodious character, creating a peaceful and reflective mood that is well-suited to the transition from day to night.

The evening hours, from 7 PM to 10 PM, are traditionally reserved for ragas such as Kafi, Bageshree, and Khamaj. These ragas often have a romantic and emotional quality, reflecting the winding down of the day and the onset of the night. Kafi, with its soft and melancholic tones, evokes a sense of longing and intimacy, making it a fitting choice for the evening.

The late night hours, from 10 PM to 1 AM, are associated with ragas like Malkauns, Darbari Kanada, and Shankara. These ragas, often composed in serious and majestic moods, reflect the stillness and depth of the night. Malkauns, with its deep and meditative tones, creates an atmosphere of introspection and spiritual contemplation, making it an ideal raga for the late night.

Finally, the midnight to pre-dawn hours, from 1 AM to 4 AM, are reserved for ragas such as Sohini, Bairagi, and Jog. These ragas, with their ethereal and mystical qualities, evoke the mystery and quiet of the midnight hours. Sohini, known for its delicate and intricate melodies, creates a dreamlike and otherworldly atmosphere, perfect for the stillness and solitude of the night.

In the Carnatic tradition, the concept of time theory, although less rigid than in Hindustani music, also plays a significant role. Certain ragas are traditionally performed at specific times to enhance their emotional impact. For example, ragas like Bowli and Revagupti are considered suitable for the early morning, while ragas like Mohanam and Shankarabharanam are typically performed in the evening. The selection of ragas based on the time of day in Carnatic music is guided by the same principles of aligning the music with the natural rhythms and moods of the day.

The scientific basis for the time theory of ragas can be understood through the study of the physiological and psychological effects of music. Research has shown that music can influence various aspects of human physiology, including heart rate, blood pressure, and brain activity. Different musical notes and rhythms can evoke different emotional and psychological responses. The time theory of ragas leverages these effects to create an optimal listening experience that resonates with the listener's state of mind and environment at different times of the day.

For musicians, adhering to the time theory of ragas requires a deep understanding of the emotional and aesthetic characteristics of each raga, as well as the ability to convey these effectively in performance. This understanding is developed through years of rigorous training and practice under the guidance of experienced gurus. The practice of performing ragas at specific times also helps musicians connect more deeply with the natural world and the rhythms of life, enhancing their own emotional and spiritual growth.

For listeners, experiencing ragas at their prescribed times can be a deeply enriching and transformative experience. The alignment of the music with the natural rhythms of the day enhances the emotional and spiritual impact of the raga, creating a profound sense of connection and harmony with the world. This connection is further deepened by the shared cultural and historical context of the ragas, which have been passed down through generations and continue to be an integral part of Indian musical heritage.

In modern times, the adherence to the time theory of ragas has faced challenges due to the demands of contemporary life and the global nature of Indian classical music. Concerts and performances are often scheduled based on convenience and availability, rather than the traditional time slots for specific ragas. However, many musicians and connoisseurs continue to value and uphold this tradition, recognizing its importance in preserving the authenticity and depth of Indian classical music.

Technological advancements and the global reach of Indian classical music have also created opportunities for innovative approaches to the time theory of ragas. Online platforms and digital recordings allow listeners to access and experience ragas at their prescribed times, regardless of geographical location. This accessibility has helped to keep the tradition alive and relevant in a rapidly changing world.

In conclusion, the time theory of ragas is a fundamental aspect of Indian classical music that enhances the emotional and spiritual experience for both performers and listeners. By aligning specific ragas with the natural rhythms and moods of the day, this tradition creates a deep sense of connection and harmony with the world. Despite the challenges posed by modern life, the adherence to the time theory of ragas remains a cherished practice that continues to enrich and inspire the world of Indian classical music. Through understanding, appreciation, and innovative approaches, this timeless tradition will continue to thrive and resonate with future generations.

One of the unique characteristics of Indian Classical Music is the assignment of definite times of the day and night for performing or listening Raga melodies. It is believed that only in this period the Raga appears to be at the height of its melodic beauty and majestic splendor. There are some Ragas which are very attractive in the early hours of the mornings; others which appeal in the evenings, yet others which spread their fragrance only near the midnight hour.

This connection of time of the day or night, with the Raga or Raginis is based on daily cycle of changes that occur in our own body and mind which are constantly undergoing subtle changes. Different moments of the day arouse and stimulate different moods and emotions.

Each Raga or Ragini is associated with a definite mood or sentiment that nature arouses in human beings. The ancient musicologists were particularly interested in the effects of musical notes, how it affected and enhanced human behavior. Music had the power to cure, to make you feel happy, excited, keep you calm, balance your mind and so on. Extensive research was carried out to find out these effects. This formed the basis of time theory as we know it today.

Emotions, feelings and thoughts have been reported to be greatly influenced by music listening or participation. Emotional experience derived from music has a powerful effect on the formation of one's moral and intellectual outlook. Music activities enhance imagination & creative thinking.

Here is an attempt to list the ragas with their therapeutically effects and the appropriate time at which these ragas should be listened. Most of the raga timings given here are taken from various sources.

The 24 hour period is divided into 8 beats each three hours long, as follows:

1. 7 a.m. – 10 a.m. first beat of the day. Daybreak; Early Morning; Morning;
2. 10 a.m. – 1 p.m. 2nd beat of the day. Late Morning; Noon; Early Afternoon;
3. 1 p.m. – 4 p.m. 3rd beat of the day. Afternoon; Late Afternoon;
4. 4 p.m. – 7 p.m. 4th beat of the day. Evening Twilight; Dusk (sunset); Early Evening;
5. 7 p.m. – 10 p.m. first beat of the night. Evening; Late Evening;
6. 10 p.m. – 1 a.m. 2nd beat of the night. Night; Midnight;
7. 1 a.m. – 4 a.m. 3rd beat of the night. Late Night
8. 4 a.m. – 7 a.m. 4th beat of the night. Early Dawn; Dawn (before sunrise); Morning Twilight

Ragas are closely related to different parts of the day according to changes in nature and development of a particular emotion, mood or sentiment in the human mind. Music is considered the best tranquillizer in modern days of anxiety, tension and high blood pressure.

Simply defined, *Raga Chikitsa* (therapy) means "healing through the use of raga." *Raga Chikitsa* is defined as "the knowledge of how to use raga for the purposes of healing". Fundamental features of *Raga Chikitsa* is the classification of the ragas based on their elemental composition (ether, air, fire, water, earth) and the proper use of the elements to balance the nature of the imbalance.

It is believed that the human body is dominated by the three *Dosha*s (three bodily humors) – *Kaph*, *Pitta* and *Vata*.

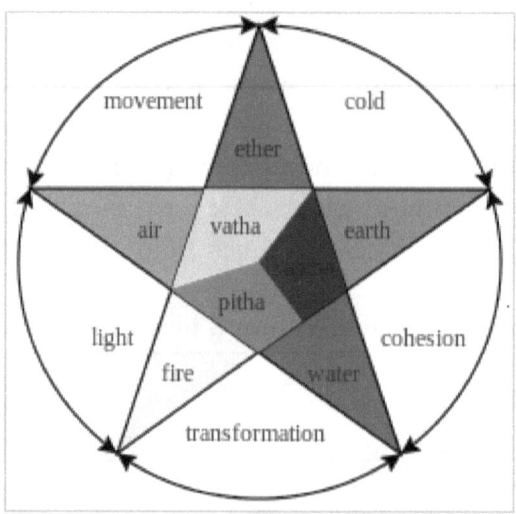

The three '*doshas*' and the five great elements they are composed from

These elements work in a cyclic order of rise and fall during the 24 hour period. Also, the reaction of these three elements differ with the seasons. Hence it is said that performing or listening to a raga at the proper allotted time can affect the health of human beings.

Raga and its Effects (Both from Hindustani and Carnatic)

Raga Kafi – Evokes a humid, cool, soothing and deep mood.

Raga Pooriya Dhansari (Hamsanandi-Kamavardini) – Evokes sweet, deep, heavy and cloudy and stable state of mind and prevents acidity.

Raga Mishra Mand – Has a very pleasing refreshing light and sweet touch.

Raga Bageshri – Arouses a feeling of darkness, stability, depths and calmness. This raga is also used in treatment of diabetes and hypertension.

Raga Darbari (Darbari Kanada) – Is considered very effective in easing tension. It is a late night raga composed by Tansen for Akbar to relieve his tension after hectic schedule of the daily court life.

Raga Bhupali and Todi – Give tremendous relief to patients of high blood pressure.

Raga Ahir-Bhairav (Chakravakam) – Is supposed to sustain chords which automatically brings down blood pressure. Controls Indigestion, Rheumatic Arthritis and Hypertension.

Raga Malkauns and Raga Asawari (Natabhairavi) – Helps to cure low blood pressure.

Also to build confidence.

Raga Tilak-Kamod (Nalinakanti), Hansdhwani, Kalavati, Durga (Suddha Saveri) -Evoke a very pleasing effect on the nerves.

Raga Bihag, Bahar (Kanada), Kafi & Khamaj - For patients suffering from insomnia and need a peaceful sonorous sleep. Useful in the treatment of sleep disorders.

Raga Bhairavi - Provides relief T.B, Cancer, Severe Cold, Phlegm, Sinus, toothache, Rheumatic Arthritis and Sinusitis. It also encourages detachment.

Raga Malhar – Useful in the treatment of asthma and sunstroke.

Raga Todi, Poorvi & Jayjaywanti – Provides relief from cold and headache.

Raga Hindol & Marava - These ragas are useful in blood purification.

Raga Shivaranjani – Useful for memory problems.

Raga Kharahara Priya - Strengthens the mind and relieves tension. Curative for heart disease and nervous irritability, neurosis, worry and distress.

Raga Hindolam and Vedanta - gives relief from '*Vatha Roga*', B.P. and Gastritis and purifies blood.

Raga Saranga – Cures '*Pitta Roga*'.

Raga Natabhairavi – Cures headache and psychological disorders.

Raga Punnagavarali, Sahana – Controls Anger and brings down violence.

Raga Dwijavanthi – Quells paralysis and sic orders of the mind.

Raga Ganamurte – Helpful in diabetes.

Raga Kapi – Sick patients get over their depression, anxiety. Reduces absent mindedness

Raga Ranjani – Helps to cure kidney disorders

Raga Rathipathipriya – Adds strength and vigor to a happy wedded life. This 5-swara raga has the power to eliminate poverty. The '*prayoga*' (implication) of the '*swara*'s can wipe off the vibrations of bitter feelings emitted by ill will.

Raga Shanmukhapriya - Instills courage in one's mind and replenishes the energy in the body.

Raga Sindhubhairavi – For a Healthy Mind and Body, Love & Happiness, Gentleness, Peace & Tranquility, Serenity.

Raga Hameerkalyani – This particular Hindusthani coloured raaga, one with great therapeutic value relaxes tension with its calming effect and brings down BP to normal 120/80.

Raga Brindavana Saranga – For Wisdom, Success, Knowledge, Joyfulness and Greater Energy.

Raga Mohana – Useful for the treatment of migraine headache.

Ragas Charukesi, Kalyani (all time raga), Sankarabharanam (evening raga) and Chandrakauns is considered very helpful for heart ailments.

Raga Ananda Bhairavi - Suppresses stomach pain in both men and women. Reduces kidney type problems. Controls blood pressure.

Raga Amrutavarshini – Ushana vyathi nasini (alleviates diseases related to heat).

Raga Reethigowla - A raga that bestows direction when one seeks it.

Raga Madhyamavati – Clears paralysis, giddiness, pain in legs/hands, etc. and nervous complaints.

Raga Bageshri – Cures insomnia.

Raga Basant Bahar – For curing Gall Stones (Cholecystitis).

Raga Bhim palasi - Gives relief from Anxiety and Hypertension.

Raga Chandrakauns - Anorexia - Heart Ailments

Raga Darbari / Darbari Kanada - Easing Tension, Headache and Asthma

Raga Deepak - Indigestion, Anorexia, Hyperacidity, Gall Stones (Cholecystitis)

Raga Gujari Todi - Cough

Raga Gunakali - Rheumatic Arthritis, Constipation, Headache, Piles or Hemorrhoids

Raga Hindol - Rheumatic Arthritis, Backache and Hypertension

Raga Jaunpuri - Intestinal Gas, Diarrhea and Constipation

Raga Jaijawanti - Rheumatic Arthritis, Diarrhoea and Headache

Raga Kafi - Sleep disorders

Raga Kausi Kanada – Hypertension and Common Cold

Raga Kedar - Headache, Common Cold and Cough, Asthma

Raga Khamaj - Sleep disorders

Raga Madhuvanti - Piles or Hemorrhoids

Raga Malkauns - Intestinal Gas - Low BP

Raga Marwa - Indigestion Hyperacidity

Raga Nat Bhairav - Indigestion, Rheumatic Arthritis, Colitis

Raga Puriya - Colitis, Anemia, Hypertension

Raga Puriya Dhanashri - Anemia

Raga Ramkali – Colitis, Piles

Raga Shree - Anorexia, Common Cold and Cough, Asthma

Raga Shudh Sarang – Anorexia, Gall Stones (Cholecystitia)

Raga Shyam Kalyan - Cough, Asthma

Raga Sohani/ Sohini - Headache

Raga Yaman - Rheumatic Arthritis

Raga Tilak Kamod - Relaxation & Easing
Raga Hansadhwani - Tension, Pleasing effect on Nerves.
Raga Kalavati, Durga, Bihag - Sonorous sleep
Raga Bhupal Todi - High Blood Pressure

The power of musical vibrations connects in some manner all things and all beings and all beings in the universe on all plants of existence. The human body has 72,000 astral nerves (*'Nadi'*) which incessantly vibrate in a specific rhythmic pattern. Disturbance in their rhythmic vibration is the root cause of disease. The musical notes restore their normal rhythm, there by bringing about good health.

Apart from the classical ragas played on musical instruments, the rhythmic sounds of temple/ church bells and *'shankha'* (conch shell or bugle) produced during devotional practices have also been found to have therapeutic applications.

A research study in Berlin University showed that the vibrations of the bugle sound could destroy bacteria and germs in the surroundings. More specifically, it was found that if the *'shankha'* is played by infusing (through the mouth) twenty-seven cubic feet of air per second, within a few minutes it will kill the bacteria in the surrounding area of twenty-two hundred square feet and inactivate those in about four-hundred square feet area further beyond.

The entire concept of Music Therapy is experimental. For me it is a kind of YOGA, which acts upon the human organism and awakens and develops their proper functions to extent of self-realization.

Music therapy is a scientific method of effective cures of disease through the power of music. It restores, maintains and improves emotional, physiological and psychological well-being. The articulation, pitch, tone and specific arrangement of *'swara*'s (notes) in a particular raga stimulates, alleviates and cures various ailments inducing electromagnetic change in the body.

Music is basically a sound or nada generating particular vibrations which moves through the medium of ether present in the atmosphere and affects the human body. Music beats have a very close relationship with heart beats. Music having 70-75 beats per minute equivalent to the normal heart beat of 72 has a very soothing effect. Likewise rhythms which are slower than 72 beats per minute create a positive suspense on the mind and body. Rhythms which are faster than the heart rate excite and rejuvenate the body.

Research has shown us that music does have healing effects .They stimulate the brain, ease tension and remove fatigue. The effect of Music Therapy may be immediate or slow, depending upon number of factors like the subject, his mental condition, environment and the type of Music, selected for having the desired effect. Music Therapy largely depends on individual needs and taste. The concept of Music Therapy is dependent on correct intonation and right use of the basic elements of music. Such as notes (*swara*) rhythm, volume, beats, and piece of melody. There are countless 'Ragas' of course with countless characteristic peculiarities of their own. . That is why we cannot establish a particular 'Raga' for a particular disease. Different types of Ragas are applied in each different case.

CHAPTER 7

Practical Application of the Book

INDIA CAN BEST be described as a land where centuries co-exist. Apart from Ayurveda and Yoga the ancient heritage of classical music can boast of an uninterrupted flow of wisdom.

India is among those few ancient civilizations that can boast of a rich intangible heritage that is alive even today; mostly orally passed down through centuries and millennia. The performing arts constitute a large and very significant part of the living traditions of our country. Passed down from generation to generation, they form the core of the cultural and even spiritual gift that India has to offer to the world.

Below I am discussing with sum up of the whole book with respect to

(i) Personal level,
(ii) Social level and
(iii) Managerial level.

At personal level following table gives you the benefits of ragas in the relevant context.

Sl. No.	Hindustani Raga	Benefits
	Raga Bhimpalasi	Has the penetrating power to infect the human mind positively and control it for days and weeks on end.
	Raga Pooriya Dhansari (Hamsanandi-Kamavardini) –	Evokes sweet, deep, heavy, cloudy and stable state of mind and prevents acidity.

	Raga Bageshri –	Arouses a feeling of darkness, stability, depths and calmness. This raga is also used in treatment of diabetes and hypertension.
	Raga Darbari (Darbari Kanada)	Considered very effective in easing tension. It is a late night raga composed by Tansen for Akbar to relieve his tension after hectic schedule of the daily court life.
	Raga Todi	Give tremendous relief to patients of high blood pressure.
	Raga Ahir-Bhairav (Chakravakam)	It is supposed to sustain chords which automatically brings down blood pressure.
	Raga Malkauns	It helps to cure low blood pressure.
	Raga Bhairavi	Provides relief T.B, Cancer, Severe Cold, Phlegm, Sinus, toothache.
	Raga Malhar	Useful in the treatment of asthma and sunstroke.
	Raga Todi	Provides relief from cold and headache.
	Raga Hindol & Marava	These ragas are useful in blood purification.

At social level following table gives you the benefits of ragas in the relevant context.

Sl. No.	Hindustani Raga	Benefits
12.	Mohana and Shivaranjani ragas	Thease may use for appreciation in studies.
13.	Raga Ananda Bhairavi	Post-Operative Pain Relief Management

The book "Raga, Yoga, and Management," delves into the intriguing intersection of Indian classical music, the practice of yoga, and modern management principles. This book presents a novel approach to personal and organizational development, emphasizing how the principles of ragas (melodic frameworks in Indian classical music) and yoga can be applied to enhance management practices, foster a harmonious work environment, and promote overall well-being. The practical application of this book's insights can be explored through various dimensions, including stress management, leadership development, team dynamics, and personal growth.

One of the key practical applications of "Raga, Yoga, and Management" is in the realm of stress management. In today's fast-paced corporate environment, stress is a pervasive issue that affects employee productivity, mental health, and overall organizational performance. The book suggests that the principles of ragas and yoga can be effectively utilized to mitigate stress and promote a sense of calm and balance. For instance, specific ragas are known to have calming effects on the mind and body. Listening to or practicing these ragas during stressful periods can help employees relax and rejuvenate. For example, Raga Yaman, with its serene and soothing melodies, can be used during break times or as background music in offices to create a tranquil atmosphere.

In addition to ragas, the incorporation of yoga practices into the workplace can significantly enhance stress management. Yoga techniques such as pranayama (breath control), meditation, and asanas (physical postures) can be integrated into daily routines to help employees manage stress more effectively. For instance, companies can organize short yoga sessions or meditation breaks during the workday, providing employees with tools to calm their minds, reduce tension, and improve concentration. These practices not only alleviate stress but also enhance overall well-being, leading to a more positive and productive work environment.

Leadership development is another crucial area where the principles outlined in "Raga, Yoga, and Management" can be applied. Effective leadership requires a combination of emotional intelligence, clarity of mind, and the ability to inspire and motivate others. The book highlights how the discipline and mindfulness cultivated through the practice of yoga can enhance leadership qualities. Yoga promotes self-awareness, emotional regulation, and mental clarity, all of which are essential attributes of a good leader. By incorporating yoga into their routines, leaders can develop greater resilience, patience, and empathy, enabling them to navigate challenges more effectively and foster a supportive and motivating work environment.

Moreover, the concept of ragas can be applied to leadership in a metaphorical sense. Just as a raga requires a deep understanding of its structure and the ability to improvise within its framework, effective leadership requires a balance of strategic thinking and adaptability. Leaders can draw inspiration from the fluidity and creativity inherent in ragas to develop a flexible and dynamic approach to management. This involves being open to new ideas, adapting to changing circumstances, and encouraging innovation within the team. By embracing these principles, leaders can create a culture of continuous learning and growth, driving organizational success.

The principles of ragas and yoga also offer valuable insights into team dynamics and collaboration. A harmonious raga performance requires the coordinated efforts of all musicians, each contributing their unique skills while being attuned to the overall composition. Similarly, effective teamwork in an organizational context requires collaboration, mutual respect, and a shared sense of purpose. The book suggests that understanding and applying the principles of harmony and balance from ragas can enhance team cohesion and performance.

For example, regular team-building activities that incorporate elements of music and yoga can strengthen interpersonal relationships and foster a sense of unity. Musical activities such as group singing or drumming circles can help team members develop a deeper sense of connection and collaboration. Similarly, group yoga sessions can promote physical and mental well-being while encouraging a spirit of camaraderie. These activities not only enhance teamwork but also create a more positive and supportive work environment, where employees feel valued and motivated.

Personal growth and self-development are fundamental aspects of the teachings in "Raga, Yoga, and Management." The book emphasizes the importance of self-awareness, mindfulness, and continuous improvement, principles that are central to both yoga and the practice of ragas. For individuals, integrating these practices into their daily lives can lead to significant personal transformation. Regular practice of yoga enhances physical health, mental clarity, and emotional stability, providing a strong foundation for personal and professional growth.

Similarly, engaging with Indian classical music, whether through listening, learning, or performing, can be a deeply enriching experience. Music has the power to evoke emotions, inspire creativity, and provide a sense of fulfilment. By exploring the world of ragas, individuals can develop a deeper appreciation for the nuances of music, enhance their emotional intelligence, and find a source of joy and relaxation. This holistic approach to personal growth, combining the physical, mental, and emotional dimensions, aligns with the principles of yoga and music therapy.

The integration of these practices into organizational culture can also lead to more sustainable and ethical management practices. The principles of yoga, such as non-violence (ahimsa), truthfulness (satya), and self-discipline (tapas), can guide ethical decision-making and foster a culture of integrity and accountability. By promoting values-based leadership and ethical behaviour, organizations can build trust with stakeholders, enhance their reputation, and achieve long-term success.

Furthermore, the book highlights the importance of mindfulness and presence in effective management. Mindfulness, a core principle of yoga, involves being fully present and engaged in the current moment. In a management context, mindfulness can enhance decision-making, improve focus, and reduce errors. Techniques such as mindful breathing, body scanning, and mindful listening can be incorporated into meetings, decision-making processes, and everyday interactions to promote a culture of mindfulness and attentiveness. This not only enhances individual performance but also contributes to a more thoughtful and deliberate organizational culture.

Another practical application of the book's insights is in enhancing creativity and innovation within organizations. The improvisational nature of ragas, which requires creativity and spontaneity within a structured framework, can serve as a metaphor for fostering innovation in the workplace. Encouraging employees to think creatively, experiment with new ideas, and take calculated risks can lead to innovative solutions and breakthroughs. By creating an environment that values creativity and supports innovative thinking, organizations can stay competitive and adapt to changing market dynamics.

The book also underscores the importance of work-life balance, a critical factor in maintaining employee well-being and productivity. The principles of yoga advocate for balance and harmony in all aspects of life. Organizations can support work-life balance by promoting flexible work arrangements, encouraging regular breaks, and providing resources for stress management and self-care. By prioritizing employee well-being, organizations can reduce burnout, enhance job satisfaction, and improve overall performance.

Incorporating the teachings of "Raga, Yoga, and Management" into corporate training programs can also yield significant benefits. Training programs that include modules on yoga, mindfulness, and music therapy can equip employees with practical tools for managing stress, enhancing focus, and improving emotional intelligence. Workshops and seminars led by experts in these fields can provide valuable insights and techniques that employees can apply in their personal and professional lives. This holistic approach to training and development can foster a more engaged, resilient, and high-performing workforce.

Moreover, the book's insights can be applied to enhance organizational culture and employee engagement. A culture that values holistic well-being, ethical behaviour, and continuous learning creates a positive and motivating environment for employees. Initiatives such as wellness programs, ethical leadership training, and opportunities for creative expression can strengthen employee engagement and loyalty. By aligning organizational practices with the principles of ragas and yoga, companies can create a supportive and inspiring workplace that attracts and retains top talent.

In conclusion, "Raga, Yoga, and Management" offers a unique and insightful approach to personal and organizational development by integrating the principles of Indian classical music, yoga, and modern management. The practical application of these principles can enhance stress management, leadership development, team dynamics, personal growth, and overall organizational well-being. By embracing these holistic practices, individuals and organizations can achieve greater harmony, balance, and success in their personal and professional endeavours. Through the thoughtful integration of ragas and yoga into daily routines and corporate practices, we can foster a more mindful, creative, and ethical world of work, where well-being and productivity go hand in hand.

Science says Art will make the kids better thinkers and nicer people. A new study supports our hunch that kids who are exposed to the arts gain benefits beyond just being "more creative."

For the students, to introduce the enlightening book "Raga, Yoga, and Management" is unique and insightful work offers a profound exploration of how the principles of Indian classical music, the practice of yoga, and modern management can harmoniously blend to enhance both personal and professional life.

In today's fast-paced and often stressful environment, finding balance and cultivating inner peace is more important than ever. This book provides valuable tools and perspectives to help you manage stress, develop leadership qualities, foster teamwork, and pursue personal growth. The integration of ragas and yoga into your daily routines can lead to a more fulfilling and productive life, both academically and beyond.

Key Takeaways:

1. **Stress Management:** Learn how specific ragas and yoga practices can help you manage stress and create a sense of calm and balance, essential for maintaining focus and mental health.
2. **Leadership Development:** Discover how the mindfulness and discipline cultivated through yoga can enhance your leadership skills, helping you to inspire and guide others effectively.
3. **Team Dynamics:** Understand the importance of harmony and collaboration, inspired by the coordinated efforts in a raga performance, to improve teamwork and foster a supportive environment.

4. **Personal Growth:** Embrace the principles of self-awareness, mindfulness, and continuous improvement from yoga and music to achieve holistic personal development.
5. **Creativity and Innovation:** Explore how the improvisational nature of ragas can inspire creativity and innovative thinking, crucial for problem-solving and adapting to new challenges.
6. **Ethical Practices:** Learn how the values of yoga, such as non-violence and truthfulness, can guide ethical decision-making and build integrity in your personal and professional life.

As you delve into this book, I encourage you to reflect on how you can incorporate these principles into your daily life. Whether it's through practicing a few minutes of yoga each day, listening to soothing ragas while studying, or applying mindful leadership techniques in group projects, the lessons from this book can profoundly impact your well-being and success.

I hope "Raga, Yoga, and Management" will inspire you to find harmony and balance, not just in your studies but in all aspects of your life. Embrace this opportunity to enrich your mind, body, and spirit, and let the wisdom of ragas and yoga guide you on your journey.

Happy reading and best wishes for your journey of self-discovery and growth!

ABOUT THE AUTHOR

Dr. Partha Priya Das is an Associate Professor at Arka Jain University, Jamshedpur, with a rich background in Commerce, Management, and Music. Holding a Ph.D. from Ranchi University, he has a diverse educational background, including LLB, B.Ed, MA-Edu, MBA, and M.Mus. He is a faculty member in the Performing Arts Department, specializing in Tabla and indian classical Guitar, at The Tagore Society, Jamshedpur. A silver medalist in Tabla and Guitar from Prayag Sangeet Samiti, he has over three decades of experience teaching and researching. Dr. Das has presented papers at national and international conferences, published articles in reputed journals, and authored book chapters. His research interests include globalization's impact on private enterprises, and he is pursuing a Ph.D. in Music. Dr. Das is also actively involved in extracurricular activities, including serving as a faculty member in performing arts and participating in cultural festivals.

Dr. Moni Deepa Das is an Assistant Professor in Commerce at Jamshedpur Worker's College, with extensive experience in teaching at various institutions. Holding a Ph.D. from Ranchi University, she has a diverse educational background, including LLB, B.Ed, MARD, MBA, and M.Mus. She is a faculty member in the Performing Arts Department, specializing in Kathak, at The Tagore Society and Sangeet Kala Kendra. Dr. Das has published numerous articles and book chapters, and she serves as an external examiner for Prayag Sangeet Samiti. Her research focuses on harmonization in accounting standards. She is also actively involved in extracurricular activities, including serving as a faculty member in performing arts and participating in cultural festivals.

www.ingramcontent.com/pod-product-compliance
Lightning Source LLC
Chambersburg PA
CBHW030931180526
45163CB00002B/524